About Demos

Demos is a greenhouse for new ideas which can improve the quality of our lives. As an independent think tank, we aim to create an open resource of knowledge and learning that operates beyond traditional party politics.

We connect researchers, thinkers and practitioners to an international network of people changing politics. Our ideas regularly influence government policy, but we also work with companies, NGOs, colleges and professional bodies.

Demos knowledge is organised around five themes, which combine to create new perspectives. The themes are democracy, learning, enterprise, quality of life and global change.

But we also understand that thinking by itself is not enough. Demos has helped to initiate a number of practical projects which are delivering real social benefit through the redesign of public services.

We bring together people from a wide range of backgrounds to cross-fertilise ideas and experience. By working with Demos, our partners develop a sharper insight into the way ideas shape society. For Demos, the process is as important as the final product.

www.demos.co.uk

First published in 2004
© Demos
Some rights reserved – see copyright licence for details

ISBN 1 84180 118 6
Typeset by Land & Unwin, Bugbrooke
Printed by Hendy Banks, London

For further information and
subscription details please contact:

Demos
The Mezzanine
Elizabeth House
39 York Road
London SE1 7NQ

telephone: 020 7401 5330
email: hello@demos.co.uk
web: www.demos.co.uk

Network Logic

Who governs in an interconnected world?

Edited by
Helen McCarthy
Paul Miller
Paul Skidmore

DEM⊙S

DEMOS

Contents

Acknowledgements

We are grateful to the National College for School Leadership for supporting this publication, and to all the authors who generously agreed to contribute essays. We would like to thank in particular Karen Stephenson for her helpful comments and support for the project.

Many individuals at Demos helped to make this collection happen, not least Tom Bentley who has provided guidance and direction throughout. Matthew Horne made important contributions at the development and commissioning stages, and Julia Huber provided crucial editing support. We must also thank Eddie Gibb for his input in the final stages and Bobby Webster, who saw the collection through to production.

As usual, all remaining errors or omissions remain our own.

Helen McCarthy
Paul Miller
Paul Skidmore
March 2004

We are some way from being able to structure public and organisational power in ways which really harness network potential . . .

Introduction

Helen McCarthy, Paul Miller
and Paul Skidmore

DEM☺S

1. Introduction

network logic

Helen McCarthy, Paul Miller and Paul Skidmore

Networks are the language of our times. Think about Al-Qaeda. The internet, eBay, Kazaa. The mobile phone, SMS. Think about iron triangles and old school ties, No Logo and DeanforAmerica. Think VISA and Amex, the teetering electricity grid, the creaking rail network. LHR to LAX. Think about six degrees of separation. Think small worlds, word of mouth.

Think about your networks. Your friends, your colleagues, your social circle. How new networks take shape through introductions at parties, over coffee breaks, via email. How your connections have helped you, supported you and hindered you.

They are all around us. We rely on them. We are threatened by them. We are part of them. Networks shape our world, but they can be confusing: no obvious leader or centre, no familiar structure and no easy diagram to describe them. Networks self-organise, morphing and changing as they react to interference or breakdown.

Networks are the language of our times, but our institutions are not programmed to understand them.

As individuals, we have taken advantage of the new connections: to earn, learn, trade and travel. But collectively we don't understand their logic. Our leaders and decision-makers have often failed to grasp their significance or develop adequate responses. We do not know how to avoid internet viruses or manage mass migration, structure urban communities, regulate global financial markets or combat networked terror.

So now we live in a world held together by networks, but lacking the language to solve its common problems. We're left with a sense of unease – a governance gap that needs to be bridged. This book brings together some of the leading network thinkers and practitioners to help us to do just that.

A new logic

Manuel Castells, in his afterword (see chapter 17), points out that we are paying so much attention to networks now because of computerisation; it is electronic connections that have made the network such a ubiquitous and public organising principle. But as both Fritjof Capra and Karen Stephenson argue in their essays, these forms go far beyond the digital. Networks embody a set of fundamental principles for the ordering, distribution and coordination of different components, whether chemical, natural, social or digital. Network principles help to explain not just the distribution of wealth in monetary economies, but also the distribution of molecules in cellular systems. If we can recognise and detect these patterns more accurately, we could learn to use them for organisation and decision-making, to make possible new forms of coordination and collective action.

There is already a huge appetite for understanding the 'hidden connections' in the world around us, as the combined book sales of our authors would testify. But we are some way from being able to structure organisational and public power in ways that really take advantage of network potential. As Capra puts it, we need new 'design principles for our future social institutions'.

Whether it is harnessing the distributed processing power of millions of networked computers as John Taylor envisages, or using Robert Sampson's penetrating analysis of crime in the modern city to activate problem-solving neighbourhood networks, there are opportunities and challenges for governments, businesses and citizens alike. Meeting them means redefining many of the principles that currently hold our world of public institutions and assumptions together. In the rest of this essay we examine the implications for some of these key principles:

- O communication
- O transparency
- O knowledge
- O innovation
- O regulation
- O accountability
- O ownership
- O citizenship
- O power.

Communication

The networks that have changed our lives most in the last two decades have been communication networks, especially the internet and mobile technologies. The most important shift is away from broadcast (one to many) towards conversational (many to many) models of communication. The music industry is not alone in finding this new era of horizontal, peer-to-peer communication uncomfortable. No major politician, with the partial exception of Howard Dean, has yet grasped the possibilities of the internet as an organising, fundraising and communicating tool in the way that Franklin Roosevelt mastered the fireside radio chat or John F Kennedy the relaxed television address. Political communication for the internet age has yet to truly arrive.

The media itself faces significant new challenges, not least from the explosion in self-publishing that new media permit. The Monica Lewinsky scandal that engulfed the Clinton presidency was initiated by an ostensibly fly-by-night website called the Drudge Report. In the Iraq conflict the controversy over 'embedding' mainstream journalists in operational military units, and the accusation that this enabled the military to filter what was and was not witnessed, played out in parallel with the highly personal missives of the 'Baghdad Blogger'. An anonymous middle-class Iraqi calling himself Salam Pax and running a weblog called DearRaed attracted global interest for the real-time, authentic, and somehow more objective perspective he appeared to offer.

Among organisations for whom the careful manipulation and transmission of images and messages is a fine art, there is much to be unlearnt. Critically, they will have to look for ways to insert themselves effectively into ongoing conversations, which they can shape and influence but probably not control. Understanding the way that messages are communicated and spread horizontally across networks is becoming more and more highly prized in this regard, as the immense popularity of Malcolm Gladwell's *The Tipping Point* demonstrates. In their essays, Ann Lieberman, Diane Wood and David Hargreaves explore the possibilities of lateral networking and collaboration between teachers to spread good practice rapidly across school systems. It will be interesting to watch the way that individuals and organisations who are seen to act 'gatekeepers' or 'hubs' in influencing people's behaviour are identified and enrolled by governments keen to influence the actions of citizens or the performance of public services, by campaigners wanting to rally people to a cause, or by companies hoping to sell them a product. Shoshana Zuboff and James Maxmin forecast a bright future for those firms trusted by consumers to act as brokers, stitching together personalised combinations of goods and services from a diverse network of providers.[1]

Transparency

In a hyperconnected society, secrets get everywhere. Transparency has gone from being something that institutions permit to something that they find it hard to resist. A misplaced click of a mouse, a careless conversation, and secrets are transmitted round the world in a matter of seconds and reported globally within hours. Wave after wave of scandals, from Iran-Contra to BSE to Enron, have illustrated the problems that a lack of transparency can create. Each has prompted policy-makers to extend powers of scrutiny so that such obliquity will not be repeated.

The dynamic of information in a network is one of openness. As Stewart Brand puts it: 'Information wants to be free.' It would be hard to overestimate the challenge that this poses. Access to information is an important source of power for professionals and organisations of every stripe, and many institutional cultures have been built on secrecy and insularity. The recent Hutton Inquiry process was remarkable less for its final outcome than for what it revealed about the machinations of Whitehall.

With the right kinds of transparency, it could be possible to rebuild public trust in institutions that have taken a battering over recent decades, but also to improve organisational performance itself. Take government policy-making, for example. The image of policy as a rigid, linear production line from 'conception' to 'winning support' to 'implementation' could evolve into something much more interactive and adaptable. Policy could be developed through genuine dialogue, tried out in small-scale ways and adapted in light of the results. Implementation on a larger scale would not follow until evidence about what worked had been clearly marshalled. Citizens would be less the passive arbiters of government performance and more the active co-creators of new policy. Such an approach would have to be accompanied by a different set of expectations, however, among both public and media. All institutions make mistakes, and good decisions depend on the capacity to consider a wide range of options. Without the scope to do so without scandal or sensation, secrecy will remain a default position among governments.

Knowledge

Brand also argued that information equally wanted to be expensive, because at the right time and in the right place it was so immeasurably valuable. This tension, and its specific application in debates ranging from intellectual property and scientific publishing to research and development and human capital banking, will manifest itself more and more frequently in the future.

The 'open source' movement has shown that it is possible, given the increased capacity for coordination that new communication networks permit, to create popular, robust and user-focused goods and services by tapping into the collaborative instincts of humans as social animals, not merely our competitive instincts as rational economic calculators. An approach that originated in software programming through things like the Linux computer operating system has now been successfully applied in the pharmaceutical industry and other knowledge-intensive sectors. Former BBC Director-General Greg Dyke announced plans to make the entire BBC archive available free online, opening up the possibility of an open source approach to broadcast content. The Creative Commons movement has sought to anchor these developments in an evolving statement of shared values and legal principles.

Yet despite its attractions the open source model has certain features that may reduce its applicability to wider social and economic endeavours. Most obviously, it depends on restricting participation to those with high levels of technical knowledge, and through a combination of peer review and central coordination it has a relatively clear mechanism for validating this knowledge. Where these conditions do not apply, then it will be crucial that we develop much more sophisticated systems of human capital banking for certifying what people know, and allowing us to find out which people know what. This is not just a challenge for governments, since the task of certifying knowledge must be distributed across the domains in which that knowledge is acquired and deployed. Instead, as Riel Miller has argued, it should be seen as a long-term collective project analogous in difficulty and importance to the development of a reliable financial capital banking system.[2]

Innovation

As a growing body of research makes clear, innovation is not a lonely process undertaken by 'Freds in sheds'. It is itself a network endeavour.[3] Good ideas are dependent on an environment that is supportive of collaboration. Partly this is about getting the right mix of people, skills and experience. American professor Richard Florida has argued that diversity and difference are often crucial attractors of creative people to high-performing cities.[4]

But these networks of innovation must also be managed and shaped to achieve longer-term public benefits. A key feature seems to be a hybrid, tight–loose approach: a tight, potentially even prescriptive approach to developing the simple rules or common standards to which all parties will work combined with a much looser approach to specifying the particular applications that will then emerge as a result. This reflects the fundamental point that networks provide a 'platform' for coordinating highly diverse activities, many of which are not predicted in advance. WiFi, SMS, even the internet itself all evolved quite differently from how they had been conceived.

Regulation

Successful innovation also depends on effective regulation. Given the benefits to citizens and consumers in terms of the goods and services that networks provide, and the potential incentives for actors to exploit their position within the network to behave in ways that reduce these benefits, special attention must be paid to the peculiar regulatory challenges that networks create. In particular, it is often necessary to separate the regulation of the 'platform' that networks provide from the actual services which are delivered via that platform. The difficulties of finding an organisational model for promoting the maintenance and improvement of the post-privatisation rail network is one recent example of this. Creating a competitive market in broadband internet access given the dominance of an incumbent market player is another.[5]

Looking to the future, similar problems are looming in relation to the provision of digital television services,[6] and even the hitherto very lightly regulated internet itself. The recent stock market flotation of the web's most popular search engine Google, and the possibility that it could be acquired by a company with a vested interest in influencing its search results, was a timely reminder that in certain respects searchability of networks through transparent and reliable search engines is a public good that cannot be left simply to the market. How we approach such regulatory conundrums remains unclear, but it seems unlikely that the models we have relied on up to now will be up to the job. The role of regulatory agencies may need to shift from that of enforcement to brokerage, identifying the organisations and strategies that could be enrolled in tackling a given problem.[7]

Accountability

In an interconnected world simple chains of cause and effect are difficult to establish. Most organisations are nodes in a whole series of complex networks, some of which they may not even realise they belong to. The impact of those networks and the outcomes they produce is rarely the result of any one organisation but rather the interactions between them. At the same time, membership of such networks does not diminish the need to give account for one's actions; on the contrary, it amplifies it. A typical FTSE 100 today is now required to give account to: shareholders, and particularly the large institutional investors whose judgements are so crucial in influencing perception of company performance and management competence; the media, through which its reputation and trust-worthiness will often be mediated; an array of regulatory agencies, perhaps sector-specific, others concerned with generic issues like employment practices or health and safety; supranational bodies, including the European Union; and its wider stakeholders, including customers, suppliers, employees, NGOs and politicians.

Yet despite this complex picture, we still treat accountability as a linear process – one party being held to account by another. This is expressed in the way that the Public Accounts Committee of the House of Commons works, for example, and in the way that the scrutiny functions of regulatory agencies continue to be understood. In the future, our conception of accountability seems likely to evolve away from simple lines of answerability towards something more complex and messy, with lines of accountability that are:

O   multiple, so that any one actor was accountable to a
     number of other actors in a number of different ways

O overlapping, so that at different times in different circumstances one source of accountability might take priority, but at no point could there be no accountability at all

O based on deliberative as well as procedural processes – generating opportunities for genuine discussion and learning, rather than fostering defensive mindsets or going through the motions.

Ownership

The blurring of responsibility and the growth of organisational interdependence also force us to rethink our binary assumptions about public versus private ownership. New ways of organising and providing public goods and services have emerged, which downgrade the role of the state from that of provider to that of regulator or coordinator, and seek to draw other actors into complex webs of provision cutting across traditional institutional boundaries. This process has been theorised in the rise of 'the governance paradigm' across the social sciences. The common theme is an interest in patterns of governing that do not rest on the traditional authority of the state to coerce and command, and which involve institutions drawn from within but also beyond government.[8]

Citizenship

Network citizens understand their connections to the wider world, as well as to those in their neighbourhood. They are capable of participating in networked forms of social action, as Howard Rheingold elaborates, but they are also able to respect the informal norms of collaboration in everyday life that enhance quality of life in the terms set out by Robert Sampson. Many of our public goods rely on the network effects of individuals being prepared to act as 'co-producers' of the service they receive from the state. Networked citizens will participate in the creation of new decision-making capabilities as well as understanding their informal power and responsibilities.

Power

The changing nature of power in a network society may be the hardest nettle to grasp. As Manuel Castells explains in his afterword, power is as crucial as ever in structuring the contours of the network society. But power no longer resides in individual institutions (even states) but in what he calls the 'switchers' through which networks regulate terms of entry and privilege or exclude particular interests or positions. These structural conditions help to explain the persistence of particular kinds of systematic disadvantage even where the wider environment appears to be in flux. Mark Buchanan's cogent analysis of the network causes of income inequality illuminates this point.

It is interesting that governments have been markedly more willing to accept the logic of network power in some policy areas than in others. Faced with the current outcry over the 'outsourcing' of service employment to call centres in India and elsewhere, for example, a coherent policy response has yet to emerge. British politicians have simply reiterated the neoliberal consensus that in a global networked economy, national policy and employment priorities are inevitably subservient to investment flows that they have little or no capacity to control.[9] By contrast, on the equally thorny question of how to deal with substantially higher levels of migration from developing countries, European governments have desperately sought to shore up creaking asylum and immigration systems in order to convince hostile electorates that control is still feasible.

In the face of interdependence, neither defeatism nor control freakery is acceptable as a strategy for governance. Public intervention to pool risk, counteract economic insecurity and counteract social dislocation is becoming more, not less, necessary. The question is what kinds of public intervention are going to be both legitimate and effective. The answer, as far as we can see, is to develop institutions able to channel this interdependence in positive ways rather than be swamped by it, and which work with the grain of our desire for self-determination rather than suppress it.

In other words, if we can only connect the pursuit of freedom to systems of organisation that will not be undone by its exercise, a networked world can become a more sustainable and a more enriching place. Making it so requires us to change not just our tools of intervention, but also our ways of seeing the world. Fortunately, the connections we have forged make it possible to pursue this task together.

Notes

1   S Zuboff and J Maxmin, *The Support Economy: why corporations are failing individuals and the next stage of capitalism* (London: Allen Lane, 2003).

2   R Miller, 'Towards the learning society?' In T Bentley and J Wilsdon (eds) *The Adaptive State: strategies for personalising the public realm* (London: Demos, 2003).

3   I Tuomi, *Networks of Innovation: change and meaning in the age of the internet* (Oxford: Oxford University Press, 2002).

4   R Florida, *The Rise of the Creative Class: and how it's transforming work, leisure, community and everyday life* (New York: Perseus, 2002).

5   See J Wilsdon and D Stedman Jones, *The Politics of Bandwidth* (London: Demos, 2002).

6   B Cox, *Free for All? Public service television in the digital age* (London: Demos, 2004).

7   J Black, 'Enrolling actors in regulatory systems; examples from UK financial services regulation', *Public Law*, Spring 2003.

8   G Stoker, 'Governance as theory: five propositions', *International Social Science Journal*, no 155, March 1998.

9   As Tony Blair put it in December 2003: 'I feel desperately sorry for anyone whose job is at risk as a result of this change, but that is the way the world is today...' 'Blair warns jobs exodus part of new order', *Financial Times*, 3 Dec. 2003.

One of the most important insights of the new understanding of life is that the network is a pattern common to all life . . .

Living Networks

Fritjof Capra

DEM☉S

2. Living networks

Fritjof Capra

In recent years networks have become a major focus of attention in science, business, and also in society at large and throughout a newly emerging global culture. Within a few years the internet became a powerful global network of communications, and many of the new internet companies act as interfaces between networks of customers and suppliers. Most large corporations today are organised as decentralised networks of smaller units, connected to networks of small- and medium-sized businesses that serve as their sub-contractors and suppliers, and similar networks exist among non-profit and non-governmental organisations. Indeed, 'networking' has been one of the main activities of political grassroots organisations for many years. The environmental movement, the human rights movement, the feminist movement, the peace move-ment, and many other political and cultural grassroots movements have organised themselves as networks that transcend national boundaries.

With the new information and communication technologies, networks have become one of the most prominent social phenomena of our time. Sociologist Manuel Castells argues that the information technology revolution has given rise to a new economy, structured around flows of information, power and wealth in global financial networks. Castells also observes that, throughout society, networking has emerged as a new form of organisation of human activity, and he has coined the term 'network society' to describe and analyse this new social structure.[1]

In science, the focus on networks began in the 1920s, when ecologists viewed ecosystems as communities of organisms, linked together in network fashion through feeding relations, and used the concept of food webs to describe these ecological communities. As the network concept became more and more prominent in ecology, systemic thinkers began to use network models at all systems levels, viewing organisms as networks of cells, and cells as networks of molecules, just as ecosystems are understood as networks of individual organisms. Correspondingly, the flows of matter and energy through ecosystems were perceived as the continuation of the metabolic pathways through organisms.[2]

The 'Web of Life' is, of course, an ancient idea, which has been used by poets, philosophers, and mystics throughout the ages to convey their sense of the interwovenness and interdependence of all phenomena. In this essay I shall discuss the fundamental role of networks in the organisation of all living systems, according to complexity theory and other recent developments in the natural and social sciences, and I shall analyse the similarities and differences between biological and social networks in some detail.[3]

The nature of life

Let us begin with biology and ask: what is the essential nature of life in the realm of plants, animals, and micro-organisms? To understand the nature of life, it is not enough to understand DNA, genes, proteins, and the other molecular structures that are the building blocks of living organisms, because these structures also exist in dead organisms, for instance in a dead piece of wood or bone.

The difference between a living organism and a dead organism lies in the basic process of life – in what sages and poets throughout the ages have called the 'breath of life'. In modern scientific language, this process of life is called metabolism. It is the ceaseless flow of energy and matter through a network of chemical reactions, which enables a living organism to continually generate, repair and perpetuate itself.

There are two basic aspects to the understanding of metabolism. One is the continuous flow of energy and matter. All living systems need energy and food to sustain themselves; and all living systems produce waste. But life has evolved in such a way that organisms form ecological communities, or ecosystems, in which the waste of one species is food for the next, so that matter cycles continually through the ecosystem's food webs.

The second aspect of metabolism is the network of chemical reactions that process the food and form the biochemical basis of all biological structures, functions and behaviour. The emphasis here is on 'network'. One of the most important insights of the new understanding of life that is now emerging at the forefront of science is the recognition that the network is a pattern that is common to all life. Wherever we see life, we see networks.

Self-generation

It is important to realise that these living networks are not material structures, like a fishing net or a spider's web. They are *functional* networks, networks of relationships between various processes. In a cell, these processes are chemical reactions between the cell's molecules. In a food web, the processes are processes of feeding, of organisms eating one another. In both cases the network is a non-material pattern of relationships.

Closer examination of these living networks has shown that their key characteristic is that they are self-generating. In a cell, for example, all the biological structures – the proteins, enzymes, the DNA, the cell membrane, and so on – are continually produced, repaired and regenerated by the cellular network.[4] Similarly, at the level of a multicellular organism, the bodily cells are continually regenerated and recycled by the organism's metabolic network. Living networks are self-generating. They continually create or recreate themselves by transforming or replacing their components. In this way they undergo continual structural changes while preserving their web-like patterns of organisation.

Boundaries of identity

All living organisms have a physical boundary that discriminates between the system – the 'self', as it were, and its environment. Cells, for example, are enclosed by membranes and vertebrate animals by skins. Many cells also have other boundaries besides membranes, such as rigid cell walls or capsules, but only membranes are a universal feature of cellular life. Since its beginning, life on Earth has been associated with water. Bacteria move in water, and the metabolism inside their membranes takes place in a watery environment. In such fluid surroundings, a cell could never persist as a distinct entity without a physical barrier against free diffusion. The existence of membranes is therefore an essential condition for cellular life.[5]

A cell membrane is always active, opening and closing continually, keeping certain substances out and letting others in. In particular, the cell's metabolic reactions involve a variety of ions, and the membrane, by being semi-permeable, controls their proportions and keeps them in balance. Another critical activity of the membrane is to continually pump out excessive calcium waste, so that the calcium remaining within the cell is kept at the precise, very low level required for its metabolic functions. All these activities help to maintain the cellular network as a distinct entity and protect it from harmful environmental influences. The boundaries of living networks, then, are not boundaries of separation but boundaries of identity.

Social networks

The main goal of my research over the past ten years has been to extend the systemic conception of life to the social domain, and in my last book, *The Hidden Connections*, I discuss this extension in terms of a new conceptual framework that integrates life's biological, cognitive and social dimensions.[6] My framework rests on the assumption that there is a fundamental unity to life, that different living systems exhibit similar patterns of organisation. This assumption is supported by the observation that evolution has proceeded for billions of years by using the same patterns again and again. As life evolves, these patterns tend to become more and more elaborate, but they are always variations on the same basic themes.

The network pattern, in particular, is one of the very basic patterns of organisation in all living systems. At all levels of life the components and processes of living systems are interlinked in network fashion. Extending the systemic conception of life to the social domain, therefore, means applying our knowledge of life's basic patterns and principles of organisation, and specifically our understanding of living networks, to social reality.

However, while insights into the organisation of biological networks may help us understand social networks, we should not expect to transfer our understanding of the networks' material structures from the biological to the social domain. Social networks are first and foremost networks of communications involving symbolic language, cultural constraints, relationships of power, and so on. To understand the structures of such networks we need to use insights from social theory, philosophy, cognitive science, anthropology and other disciplines. A unified systemic framework for the understanding of biological and social phenomena will emerge only when network theories are combined with insights from these other fields of study.

Social networks, then, are not networks of chemical reactions, but networks of communications. Like biological networks, they are self-generating, but what they generate is mostly non-material. Each communication creates thoughts and meaning, which give rise to further communications, and thus the entire network generates itself.[7]

The dimension of meaning is crucial to understand social networks. Even when they generate material structures – such as material goods, artifacts or works of art – these material structures are very different from the ones produced by biological networks. They are usually produced for a purpose, according to some design, and they embody some meaning.

As communications continue in a social network, they form multiple feedback loops, which eventually produce a shared system of beliefs, explanations and values – a common context of meaning, also known as culture, which is continually sustained by further communications. Through this culture individuals acquire identities as members of the social network, and in this way the network generates its own boundary. It is not a physical boundary but a boundary of expectations, of confidentiality and loyalty, which is continually maintained and renegotiated by the network of communications.

Culture, then, arises from a network of communications among individuals; and as it emerges, it produces constraints on their actions. In other words, the rules of behaviour that constrain the actions of individuals are produced and continually reinforced by their own network of communications. The social network also produces a shared body of knowledge – including information, ideas and skills – that shapes the culture's distinctive way of life in addition to its values and beliefs. Moreover, the culture's values and beliefs also affect its body of knowledge. They are part of the lens through which we see the world.

Living networks in human organisations

In recent years it has become very popular in management circles to use metaphors like 'the living company', trying to understand a business organisation as a living, self-organising system.[8] It is therefore instructive to apply our network approach to the analysis of human organisations.

Living social systems, as we have seen, are self-generating networks of communications. This means that a human organisation will be a living system only if it is organised as a network or contains smaller networks within its boundaries, and only if these networks are self-generating. Organisational theorists today speak of 'communities of practice' when they refer to these self-generating social networks.[9] In our daily activities, most of us belong to several communities of practice – at work, in schools, in sports and hobbies, or in civic life. Some of them may have explicit names and formal structures, others may be so informal that they are not even identified as communities.

Whatever their status, communities of practice are an integral part of our lives.

As far as human organisations are concerned, we can now see that they have a dual nature. On the one hand, they are social institutions designed for specific purposes, such as making money for their shareholders, or managing the distribution of political power. On the other hand, organisations are communities of people who interact with one another to build relationships, help each other, and make their daily activities meaningful at a personal level.

This dual nature as legal and economic entities as well as communities of people derives from the fact that various communities of practice invariably arise and develop within the organisation's formal structures. These are informal networks – alliances and friendships, informal channels of communication, and other webs of relationships – which continually grow, change and adapt to new situations.

Within every organisation there is a cluster of interconnected communities of practice. The more people are engaged in these informal networks, and the more developed and sophisticated the networks are, the better will the organisation be able to learn, respond creatively to new circumstances, change and evolve. In other words, the organisation's aliveness resides in its communities of practice.

In order to maximise a company's creative potential and learning capabilities it is crucial for managers and business leaders to understand the interplay between the organisation's formal, designed structures and its informal, self-generating networks.[10] The formal structures are sets of rules and regulations that define relationships between people and tasks, and determine the distribution of power. Boundaries are established by contractual agreements that delineate well-defined subsystems (departments) and functions. The formal structures are depicted in the organisation's official documents – the organisational charts, bylaws, manuals and budgets that describe the organisation's formal policies, strategies and procedures.

The informal structures, by contrast, are fluid and fluctuating networks of communications. These communications include nonverbal forms of mutual engagement in joint enterprises, informal exchanges of skills, and the sharing of tacit knowledge. These practices create flexible boundaries of meaning that are often unspoken.

In every organisation there is a continuous interplay between its informal networks and its formal structures. The formal policies and procedures are always filtered and modified by the informal networks, which allows them to use their creativity when faced with unexpected and novel situations. Ideally, the formal organisation will recognise and support its informal networks of relationships and will incorporate their innovations into the organisation's formal structures.

Biological and social networks

Let us now juxtapose biological and social networks and highlight some of their similarities and differences. Biological systems exchange molecules in networks of chemical reactions; social systems exchange information and ideas in networks of communications. Thus, biological networks operate in the realm of matter, whereas social networks operate in the realm of meaning.

Both types of networks produce material structures. The metabolic network of a cell, for example, produces the cell's structural components, and it also generates molecules that are exchanged between the network's nodes as carriers of energy or information, or as catalysts of metabolic processes. Social networks, too, generate material structures – buildings, roads, technologies and so on – that become structural components of the network; and they also produce material goods and artefacts that are exchanged between the network's nodes.

In addition, social systems produce non-material structures. Their processes of communication generate shared rules of behaviour, as well as a shared body of knowledge. The rules of behaviour, whether formal or informal, are known as social structures and are the main focus of social science. The ideas, values, beliefs and other forms of knowledge generated by social systems constitute structures of meaning, which we may call semantic structures.

In modern societies, the culture's semantic structures are documented – that is, materially embodied – in written and digital texts. They are also embodied in artefacts, works of art and other material structures, as they are in traditional non-literate cultures. Indeed, the activities of individuals in social networks specifically include the organised production of material goods. All these material structures – texts, works of art, technologies and material goods – are created for a purpose and according to some design. They are embodiments of the shared meaning generated by the society's networks of communications.

Finally, biological and social systems both generate their own boundaries. A cell, for example, produces and sustains a membrane, which imposes constraints on the chemistry that takes place inside it. A social network, or community, produces and sustains a non-material, cultural boundary, which imposes constraints on the behaviour of its members.

Conclusion

The extension of the systemic conception of life to the social domain discussed in this essay explicitly includes the material world. For social scientists, this may be unusual, because traditionally the social sciences have not been very interested in the world of matter. Our academic disciplines have been organised in such a way that the natural sciences deal with material structures while the social sciences deal with social structures, which are understood to be, essentially, rules of behaviour.

In the future, this strict division will no longer be possible, because the key challenge of our new century – for social scientists, natural scientists and everyone else – will be to build ecologically sustainable communities.[11] A sustainable community is designed in such a way that its technologies and social institutions – its material and social structures – do not interfere with nature's inherent ability to sustain life. In other words, the design principles of our future social institutions must be consistent with the principles of organisation that nature has evolved to sustain the web of life. A unified conceptual framework for the understanding of material and social structures, such as the one offered in this essay, will be essential for this task.

Fritjof Capra, PhD, physicist and systems theorist, is a founding director of the Center for Ecoliteracy in Berkeley. He is the author of several international bestsellers, including The Tao of Physics *and* The Web of Life. *This essay is based on his most recent book* The Hidden Connections. *www.fritjofcapra.net*

Notes

1   M Castells, *The Rise of the Network Society* (Oxford: Blackwell, 1996).
2   F Capra, *The Web of Life* (London: HarperCollins, 1996).
3   For a more extensive analysis, see F Capra, *The Hidden Connections* (London: HarperCollins, 2002).
4   See H Maturana and F Varela, *The Tree of Knowledge* (Boston: Shambhala, 1987) and Capra, *Web of Life.*
5   Capra, *Hidden Connections.*
6   Ibid.
7   See N Luhmann, 'The autopoiesis of social systems' in N Luhmann (ed.) *Essays on Self-Reference* (New York: Columbia University Press, 1990) and Capra, *Hidden Connections.*
8   See, for example, A de Geus, *The Living Company* (Boston: Harvard Business School Press, 1997).
9   See E Wenger, *Communities of Practice* (Cambridge: Cambridge University Press, 1998).
10 Capra, *Hidden Connections.*
11 Ibid.

Reciprocity is key to the power of networks, the alchemy of mutual give and take over time turning to a golden trust . . .

Towards a theory of government

Karen Stephenson

DEM⊙S

3. Towards a theory of government

Karen Stephenson

Governments don't move; they morph. Built on the skeletal remains of past policies they grow incrementally like a coral reef, changing the ecosystem around them. And, like coral reefs, they are vast structures, difficult to chart thoroughly. But governments are not bureaucracies, no matter how much they may look and feel like a barrier reef at times. So what are they?

Commentators on both sides of the Atlantic have long lamented the existence of 'big government'. But size isn't everything. Sure, scale still matters: government sprawl – going from 1,000 to 50,000 to 200,000 employees – can and does make a difference. But what if there was an iterative pattern to the structuring of increasing scale? That's exactly the reason the French anthropologist Levi-Strauss once claimed to have found an 'atom' of kinship, an elementary structure common to every biological or fictive family.[1] As it turned out, his idea was more provocative than practical: there was no such reliably repeating structure. But what if there was an atom of organisation, a recurring structure of how people organise? And, if so, what implication does it have for leadership and governance?

Markets, hierarchies and networks

Let's try to answer these questions by starting with what we know. Assume a hierarchy. It was long thought that hierarchy was an island of planned coordination in a sea of market relationships, a pristine paradise inhabited by vertically integrated tribes of employees.[2] But corporate anthropologists debunked the myth of the CEO, the savage noble burned at the stake in a bonfire of vanities, just as British anthropologists overturned the myth of the noble savage a century before. Why? Because whether the jungles are green and leafy or concrete, they are brimming with intricate webs of relationships, which when viewed from afar reveal elementary structures.

Initially, these elementary structures were sorted into a triptych of organisational forms: markets, hierarchies and networks. Standing at one end, a chorus of economists droned 'market' as their mantra – the genesis of organisational life. On the other end perched hierarchy, the logical evolutionary endpoint, the height of civilised achievement. Networks were largely ignored or dismissed as a mixed breed, a doomed hybrid nesting somewhere between the two.

But the resulting theoretical continuum of market – network – hierarchy was misguided, as was made profoundly apparent on September 11, 2001. Networks would prove to be core to the continuum, and hierarchy the hybridised half-breed. Networks were and are deeply linked to cultural genesis and genocide, and comprise the core DNA within any governance structure.

Transaction costs and organisational form

To understand how the old continuum, though mistaken, became accepted, we start with Ronald Coase's classic paper on the nature of the firm.[3] Coase suggested that firms and markets, while different organisational structures, nevertheless share common transactional practices. The distinction, later amplified by Williamson,[4] was based on the amount of knowledge about a transaction (or 'asset specificity') that was required. Disinterested, non-repetitive exchanges occurred as market transactions (simple contracts). But exchanges that entailed greater uncertainty, and therefore a proportional amount of asset specificity, were best sheltered within the firm as a way to mitigate the greater risk.

Once these transactions were harboured in the firm, inefficiencies devolved. Williamson argued that these inefficiencies were tolerated, in fact preferred, because of the firm's own bounded rationality – better the devil you know than the devil you don't – and theories of firm and hierarchy were conceived.[5] In refining these propositions and terms a continuum of transactions emerged, beginning with the disinterested and discrete market transactions on one end and the interested, asset-specific transactions of a firm's hierarchy on the other.

Powell suggested that networks deserved a place on the continuum, for they permitted exchanges that required asset specificity but at the same time could move through semi-permeable organisational boundaries typical of family businesses, guilds and cartels.[6] Networks collide and collude and are able to elude organisational boundary 'checkpoints' nimbly because of the trust and mutual reciprocity between the actors – in essence invisibly storing the asset-specific knowledge of the transaction in the trust relationship itself.[7] Networks produce nuanced asynchronous and asymmetric exchanges, deftly avoiding both the visible hand of hierarchy[8] and the invisible hand of the market.[9]

Sounds right, feels right – but it's wrong. Let's rethink the continuum in light of the logic of exchange and put the argument right. At one extreme are disinterested, non-repetitive exchanges typically found in markets. The logical inversion would be repetitive exchanges of mutual interest evidenced in networks. Hierarchy, comprised of routine exchanges (repetitive like a network) with a governing authority (more in keeping with the contractual characteristics of market exchanges), is now squarely in the middle, having qualities of both network and market. Table 1 summarises these organisational forms and features in their logical order.

Ramifications for organisations

What does this mean for organisations? In markets, it's a 'free-for-all' – a knowledge diaspora, information spreading virally to where it is most needed regardless of legal (or moral) boundaries. But in organisations, the interests are best if not 'self' served when knowledge is more closely held because of the routine and repetitive exchanges that result from established procedures and the knowledge

Table 1 Organisational forms and their associated exchange rates

Organisational form	ABCs of exchange
Market	Disinterested, non-repetitive
Hierarchy	Routinised by a governing authority
Network	Mutually interested, repetitive

shared among those in authority. Therefore, organisations and their governance are directly shaped by only hierarchies and networks. In broad strokes, these organisational structures can be distinguished by a very simple rule of thumb. First, in a hierarchy one person can perform the work of one: work is directly related to the job assignment – one for one and one for all; second, in a network shared collective intelligence is exponential: two people can perform the work of four. This multiplier effect is a result of the leveraging of individual efforts through bonds of mutual trust and reciprocity, as evidenced by sturdy hunter-gatherers who daily survived overwhelming ecological odds through cooperation. Small groups everywhere share this ancient and larger-than-life capability with their Kalahari counterparts.

Reciprocity is key to the power of networks, exerting a governing logic over them – the alchemy of mutual give and take over time turning to a golden trust. Primordially, trust was determined through face-to-face interactions, and to a large extent is still today. Therefore one needs to appreciate the profound truth that the face of trust is still a human face, a face that can mask a fundamental fear of differences. The stark truth about trust is that if you don't look like me, or dress like me, walk or talk like I do, then I am not likely to know or understand you. This fetish for the familiar is fundamentally tribal and resistant to diversification.[10] A network of trust is the real invisible hand behind every act of deceit, fraud and betrayal. Trust is the caress of forgiveness and friendship, the unshakeable grip of family or tribe.

What happens when networks and hierarchy are misaligned? A bureaucracy is the logical but unfortunate result. Bureaucracies write over their past wrongs, exacting obedience by methodically numbing collective consciousness through the destruction or stoppage of careers. In fully mature bureaucracies, two people perform the work of one-half. This is the real truth behind budgetary shortfalls. So whether you are a hunter-gatherer or hunting and pecking your way through a bureaucracy, you are operating as you would in a network, not a market or hierarchy. Transactors and transactions change all the time in markets and hierarchies – in markets because the transactions are disinterested and non-repetitive, and in hierarchies because they are routinised regardless of who performs them. Although hierarchies are lauded, we've all heard the laughable refrain, 'I've worked for five heads of department!' Staying power is found not in who's at the top but in who's in the network.

Ramifications for government

Human networks have evolved from bands, tribes, 'segmentary lineages' and chiefdoms right up to the modern state. Government operations betray the signs of this evolutionary heritage, strikingly similar to a 'segmentary lineage' system.[11] When policies change or new needs arise, teams are created not from the ground up, but as sub-units of existing segments. As layers of hierarchy proliferate, units at each layer compete against one another, combining to work as a larger unit only when these too are drawn into competition. So within a government department one team jockeys for position with another, one directorate attacks another to protect its budget, and the department as a whole fights other departments to defend its turf. In these systems there is no internal structure or infrastructure to join the system as a whole; it is simply a network of hierarchies (vertically integrated silos). As such, they are never more than (and are often less than) the sum of their parts. Segmentary systems calculate power by comparing and contrasting their stock or status with that of other segments. Competition, not collaboration, is the watchword.

So it comes as no surprise when people in the public sector complain of being stuck in organisational 'silos', obstacles to be overcome by 'joined-up' working. What we don't realise is that we are hard-wired to create these silos because of the constraints of segmentary systems. Figure 1 shows what a segmentary system looks like depicted graphically. It is the image of an organisational analysis that was conducted of the US government, three hierarchical layers down from the president. Within each organisational box or segment you can see smaller subgroups denoted by densely connected circles. The perimeters of the circles are made up of microscopic dots denoting real people and the criss-crossing lines that fill each circle represent the reciprocal communications between the individuals in each box. It is obvious that the relative density within the boxes eclipses the connections among the boxes, indicating that people

Figure1   Segmentary lineage within the US government

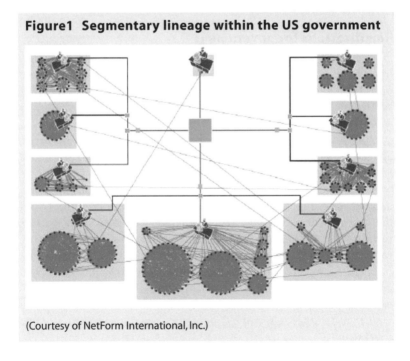

(Courtesy of NetForm International, Inc.)

spend their limited resources investing in segmentary or 'silo-ed' relationships within each box or segment. The unhappy result was that segmentary politics consisted largely of errors and their associated rework, achieved at the peril of overall organisational effectiveness.

It is easy to see from this example how segmentary politics can easily and perversely thwart overall objectives and goals. Real problems do not come neatly packaged. Whether in fighting terrorism or tackling corporate fraud, cross-cutting problems require cross-cutting solutions. Yet in segmentary systems of government there is no process in place to allow the seamless exchange of vital information laterally among the different units with an interest in tackling the problem with the knowledge or resources to do so. The result is that information disappears, deadlines are missed, fingers point and wrongs are papered over. The knowledge of how to put it right – to put a process in place – is in the networks of the people doing the work.

That is why it is important to understand the differences between how people actually work in their networks and how the process says they should work. When it was first elected, the Blair administration made much of the need for 'joined-up' working. This was exemplified by the agglomeration of several smaller departments and budgets into the giant Department for the Environment, Transport and the Regions (DETR). The failure and subsequent break-up of the DETR showed that putting people in the same building or changing the name on the signs does not automatically lead to integrated working. But this misalignment between the network of work and the formal processes is a continuous feature of every organisation, not least because market conditions are always changing and organisations are always adapting to keep up.

This phenomenon is exacerbated by the growing recognition within government of its limited capacity to tackle policy problems autonomously, and a growing desire instead to build partnerships of public, private and voluntary sector actors better equipped to address them. Are there any examples where governments are transforming the way they partner with their stakeholders? Is there an established way to benchmark these kinds of public–private collaborations?

A step in the right direction

One exciting project involves a collaboration between HM Customs and Excise, the Government Office for the East Midlands and the East Midlands Development Agency. The project is using a new technique known as virtual network analysis (VNA) to try to improve partnership working.[12] The approach combines process mapping and modelling with what is known as social network analysis, or 'people mapping'. In human networks the assets are tacit, intangible and intellectual. VNA maps and measures these intangible assets in order to make them tangible and the effective management of them more possible.

Three trials were commissioned by the Director of Crime Reduction in the East Midlands, addressing:

○   domestic violence in Northampton
○   burglary in Nottingham
○   sport partnerships in Nottinghamshire.

The VNA trials are currently in various stages of completion. Already the findings are positive. Blockages have been identified and efficient integrated working solutions are being implemented. Some improvements have been immediate; others take more time. In the domestic violence trial in Northampton, for instance, the study revealed that 'four different agencies all carrying out multi-agency training to different standards were unaware of each other's work in this area'. When these shared practices were identified, knowledge was much more effectively leveraged through group learning. In the burglary trial in Nottingham it was discovered that one crime-solving division was holding crucial knowledge close to its chest to the detriment of other parts of the organisation. Systems for effective knowledge transfer and reward mechanisms for sharing information were explored.

Looking to the future

We know from the science of networks that there is hard-wiring embedded in the apparent 'softness' of social capital. Indeed, social capital has been the missing link in a performance equation that only valued human capital as measured hierarchically. The very nature of traditional performance measures is silo-esque – people are measured by those to whom they report. Now, by combining social and human capital measures, the intellectual assets of the organisation can be asserted, assessed and quantified. People can be measured by whether they run to, not away from, problems. This recognition carries with it the potential, at the very least, to neutralise the myopic exclusivity of the silo mentality. At best, it could hold the key to neutralising the destructive networks of international crime, fraud and terrorism.

VNA is an important approach in facilitating more effective cooperation between segments, but more work lies ahead. In particular, while processes may be mapped and aligned, who is looking after the leaders? Where does the leadership reside and what does it look like? Traditional leadership theory focuses on the typical 'one leader' approach and falls short of the mark. Within a segmentary system we must rethink leadership as a network of segment leaders, cooperating and coordinating at improved efficiencies for the greater good of the total enterprise. This is true infrastructure. Figure 2, developed for the VNA trials, tries to capture this concept. In this VNA world, leaders at some time or to some degree are followers.[13] At any one time leaders may be leading:

○ laterally for external partnerships
○ laterally for internal partnerships
○ downwardly for vertically integrated hierarchies and
○ intermittently according to the exigencies of a decision
   process.[14]

The real lesson here is that the recombinant properties of a leadership network are just as important to model and understand as the processes they govern.

Figure 2 Model for government

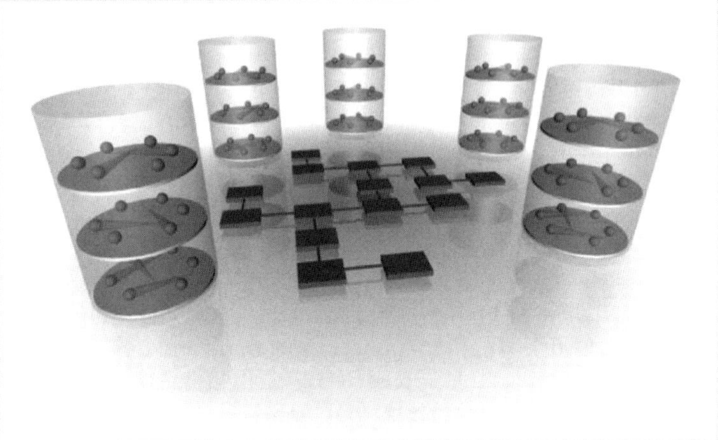

(Courtesy of Enterprise Modeller Solutions Ltd)

The key point is this: just because you have an organisational chart at your fingertips does not mean you have a charter for your world. And having the networks mapped does not tell you about the cultural terrain you have to cross in order to lead effectively; the map is most certainly not the territory. Rather it is the lack of a coordinated leadership network within a network of hierarchies that produces the lurches, lunging and sputtering we frequently experience in government. What I have tried to do here is explain the science underlying the practical vagaries, which is essential for planning and predicting effective change.

With e-government and virtual operations increasing, it becomes even more salient to have government segments coordinated for rapid learning and operational adaptation. It's difficult to resign ourselves to living in a world where even the best-intentioned can undermine or devastate operations by a simple flip of a switch. But we do live in such a world and it is filled with this kind of risk. It's up to us to engender the kind of trust and build the kind of government that will make it a better and safer place.

Karen Stephenson is professor of management at the Harvard Graduate School of Design and President of Netform, Inc. Her book The Quantum Theory of Trust *will be published by Financial Times Prentice Hall later this year.*

Notes

1   C Levi-Strauss, 'The mathematics of man', *International Social Science Bulletin*, no 6, 1955 and *The Elementary Structures of Kinship*, tr. J Harle Bell, J R von Sturmer and R Needham (Boston: Beacon Press, 1971)
2   Adapted from G B Richardson, 'The organization of industry', *Economic Journal*, no 82, 1972.
3   R Coase, 'The nature of the firm', *Economica*, no 4, 1937.
4   O Williamson, *Markets and Hierarchies* (New York: Free Press, 1975), *The Economic Institutions of Capitalism* (New York: Free Press, 1984) and 'Transaction cost economics and organization theory', *Industrial and Corporate Change*, no 2, 1993.
5   Management theorists put their imprimatur on the debate with derivative theories based on hybrid organisational forms and managerial approaches, such as the 'U' and 'M' organisation and Theories X and Y (D McGregor, 'The human side of enterprise', *Management Review*, Nov 1957) and Z (W Ouchi, *Theory Z* (New York: Addison-Wesley Publishing, 1981)) respectively.
6   W Powell, 'Neither market nor hierarchy: network forms of organization', *Organizational Behavior*, no 12, 1990.
7   M Granovetter, 'Economic action and social structure: a theory of embeddedness', *American Journal of Sociology*, no 91, 1985.
8   A Chandler, *The Visible Hand* (Cambridge, MA: Harvard University Press, 1977).
9   A Smith, *The Wealth of Nations* (Oxford: Clarendon Press, 1976).
10 K Stephenson, 'Networks', in *CRC The Technology Management Handbook,* ed. R Dorf (Boca Raton: CRC Press, 1999).
11 M Sahlins, 'The segmentary lineage: an organization for predatory expansion', *American Anthropologist*, no 63, 1961. In the early stages of human organisation leaders were typically charismatic and built a following by creating loyalties using generosity or fearful acquiescence through magic, demonstrated wisdom, oratorical skill, and so on. A change occurred between the segmentary lineage and chiefdom, where leadership was no longer carried out by a charismatic leader but by an instituted office authorised by God, coup or chad.
12 For more information see www.benchmarking.co.uk or contact Jeremy Hawkins at the East Midlands Crime Reduction Unit.

13   M Sahlins, 'Poor man, rich man, big man, chief: political types in Melanesia and Polynesia', *Comparative Studies in Society and History*, no 5, 1963.
14   Detailed in M Kriger and L Barnes, 'Executive leadership networks: top management group dynamics in a high-performance organization', in *The SYMLOG Practitioner: Applications of small group research*, eds R Polley, A Hare and P Stone (New York: Praeger, 1988).

Seeing the connectedness of things is the starting point for understanding a world that otherwise appears baffling . . .

Connexity revisited

Geoff Mulgan

DEM☉S

4. Connexity revisited

Geoff Mulgan

Connexity was published in 1997 in the UK – and has subsequently been published (and translated) in various parts of the world, from the US and Greece to China.[1] The book made three arguments.

First, that the growing connectedness of the world is the most important social and economic fact of our times. It is manifest in the growth of physical links like telecom networks; in rising flows of goods, money, ideas and people; in the interconnectedness of culture and the environment; and in new forms of social organisation. Hence the reuse of an old English word, connexity.

Second, that this connectedness renders redundant many of the dominant concepts of political, social and economic thought that assumed a world of sovereign and separate entities: nation states, companies and individual citizens. The key intellectual methods needed to understand the contemporary world, by contrast, focus on the character of systems, connections and feedback loops, and on subjects of action who are not seen as complete and bounded in the manner of nineteenth-century liberalism or twentieth-century economics.

Third, that this connectedness poses major moral challenges, above all concerning our responsibilities to others. For example, how should we rethink our consumption patterns in the light of climate change? How should we and our governments respond to genocide and failing states in distant countries? I argued that these issues were set to rise up the political agenda and would require radical changes to our institutions.

Since I wrote the book all of these trends have intensified. The world has continued becoming more connected; the boundaries between international and domestic policy have blurred irrevocably; and the gap between the scale and nature of the problems and the capacities of institutions to deal with them has grown. Within business, governments and civil society the importance of networks in helping with coordination, learning and the creation of value has become more commonplace.

Networks, hierarchies and control

Connexity built on the more theoretical account set out in an earlier book, *Communication and Control*.[2] This argued that the information revolution was best understood as an increase in capacities to control, and that these would be exploited both by new horizontal networks and by traditional hierarchies.

The empowerment of networks is becoming widely understood in everything from knowledge management to protest. Oddly, it is the empowerment of hierarchies that is now less well recognised.

For many the promise of the information revolution was that power would be distributed evenly. The network would displace the hierarchy, as in Tom Paine's marvellous description of democracy shattering the crown of royal dominion and giving each citizen a jewelled piece. A networked world would empower citizens against states, consumers against companies, the weak against the strong.

Networks can, indeed, be genuinely empowering. But some of the characteristics of knowledge – its zero marginal cost, replicability and fungibility – and some of the characteristics of networks – their reach, and exponentially rising value – have led to greater not lesser concentrations of power and have reinforced some hierarchies. The key characteristic of hierarchies is concentration: concentration of resources at the points where it can make most impact, and concentration of control over resources that others need: money, knowledge, votes, even processing power.

We still live in a world of powerful hierarchies. Governments take a larger not smaller share of GDP than they did 10 or 20 years ago. The military depend on tighter command systems than ever before to avoid mistakes, since the response of a warship to air attack now has global ramifications. Power in the global media, and power over the 'memes' that shape minds, is more concentrated than ever despite the proliferation of magazines and websites. For all the talk of the network economy most businesses are organised as fairly tight hierarchies, albeit with fewer layers, and some that used not to be, like partnerships, are taking more traditional corporate forms. Again, one of the drivers of this is globalisation, since what a subsidiary does in a distant country – using child labour, say – may have an impact on consumers here. The same is true in NGOs. Look closely at Greenpeace, for example, and you see a fairly tightly controlled hierarchy, not loose democracies. Within and around all of these are networks: networks for managing relationships, knowledge and information. But at their heart lie hierarchical organisations of power and authority able to act decisively and quickly, with concentrations of resources and with some of the properties of Bentham's panopticon, able to see everything from the centre in real time.

So although networks have become much more important to the way we live, we do not live in a world dominated by networks. Networks are extraordinary ways of organising knowledge, cooperation and exchange. They are far more effective means of sharing learning than hierarchies and generally better at adapting to change. But they remain poor at mobilising resources, sustaining themselves through hard times, generating surpluses, organising commitments, or playing games of power. This is why, for example, the interesting feature of the anti-globalisation movement is its weakness not its strength, and why Al-Qaeda can inflict huge damage but cannot create.

Risk and the state

The continuing importance of hierarchy in a networked world partly reflects the nature of risk. States have their origins as protections against risk: protection from invasion and attack, then in the nineteenth century from disease, and later still protection from poverty and unemployment. Much of what we count as progress in urbanised societies has been the increasing success of many states in protecting their citizens – from war, disease and poverty.

Some expected a networked world based on information to reverse this, or at least to offer a different way of handling risk. It is certainly harder for states to build certain kinds of walls or control what information and knowledge reaches their citizens (though the Taliban tried). The other widespread prediction was that a more networked world would inevitably encourage greater individualisation of risk, which might leave each person, or at least everyone with the means to do so, with their own insurance, purchased on global markets, calibrated using sophisticated algorithms, particularly with new genetic knowledge. People would buy their own security, education, or healthcare, as the state, and pooled risk, withered away.

The reality is very different. We remain in a world where many risks are collective and where the public rationally looks to public institutions to protect them. These include the risks of instability in the global market, the risks of attacks on systems on which we depend (from food distribution to electricity), risks to personal privacy or global warming (in each of which states can be as much the problem as the solution). Paradoxically the very speed with which networks have advanced has reinforced the need for stronger legitimate authorities to protect people from the risks they have brought in their wake.

The nature of risk also underscores the importance of moral obligations to others. September 11 was a reminder that even the richest and most powerful remain vulnerable. Thomas Hobbes's words from over 300 years ago have special resonance now. In *Leviathan* he wrote that 'the weakest has strength enough to kill the strongest, either by secret machination or by confederacy with others …', which is why the strongest need to care about the lives and needs of the weakest.

The implications of connexity

What follows for governments, whether of cities or states? In *Connexity* I set out some of the emerging principles for government – from the relationship with citizens and the role of trust to the use of more horizontal structures in bureaucracies. Five aspects stand out.

Transparency

The first is the potential for radically greater transparency because of the ease and cheapness of sharing information. On the Web I can look up my street on a site called upmystreet.com. Through it I can instantly find out information not just about local contacts or discussion groups but also about the relative performance of my local schools or local police force. I can do this because government has been through a revolution in how information is organised. Much that used to be internal, the prerogative of management, is now external. Information has been turned inside out, rather like a Richard Rogers building.

This shift was bitterly resisted by the professions and many of the experts in each field, who feared that the information was crude and that the public wouldn't be able to make sense of it. Yet having happened it is irreversible, and has turned out to be a powerful force for changing cultures of provision, driving up performance and encouraging weak performers to learn from their more successful counterparts.

Transparency has also changed the working practices of government. A good example is food, where public trust in government collapsed in the UK in the 1990s because of BSE. Now the Food Standards Agency makes all its decisions in public, publishes all the scientific and other data underpinning those decisions, and has quickly shown that a more open, adult approach increases public trust. My guess is that future governments will simply take that sort of greater transparency for granted, as an unavoidable aspect of the environment in which they have to work.

Holism

The second principle is holism: the potential for governments to see how things connect. Systems thinking, and the possibilities of networks, are together pushing towards what we call holistic, joined-up government – reversing the logic of nineteenth-century functionalism, and the logic of the new public management which divided every task into component parts, separate functions or markets. Instead, smart networks make it possible to organise the forms of government in very different ways, starting with needs, outcomes, or client groups and then working backwards to fit functions to them.

In welfare and justice, for example, the case management approach has been widely adopted, so that if a 16 year old gets into trouble the different agencies – police, social services and voluntary organisations – are brought together by a single person to fit the young person's individual needs. On the Web, government services have been clustered by life experience – such as having a baby or retiring. At a national level some budgets have been moved away from departments to cross-cutting structures – like Surestart for under-3s or the fund for conflict prevention in sub-Saharan Africa, so that the money follows the problem rather than being the preserve of departments, agencies and professions. Old-fashioned vertical hierarchies still have their place. But over time the likelihood is that horizontal, networked structures will increasingly displace them.

Directness

The third principle is directness. In the past governments had to operate through many layers of mediation, tiers and hierarchical bureaucracies. Now more direct relationships are feasible. Take health. A big advance in the UK has been NHS Direct, a 24/7 phone and online service of advice and diagnosis, which is in part about empowering individuals to take more command of their own health. If my daughter is sick at 3am I can speak to a nurse or look up guidance. The idea is not all that radical in itself. But it brings together old elements (phones and nurses) in a new way, just as printing, for example, was not a new invention but rather a combination of raised letters from coins, the wine press and etching.

Directness applies in other fields too. Learndirect and the National Grid for Learning now provide a full range of courses accessible online, with back-up from tutors both phone-based and face to face. Such approaches have the potential over time to transform education into a much more user-driven system. In the field of democracy there has been constant experimentation to increase direct engagement. In the UK one-fifth of local councils have used citizens' juries. There have been more referendums in the last seven years than in the last 70. Power has been devolved to Scotland, Wales and Northern Ireland, which now have their own very self-contained political lives. Postal voting has doubled turnouts in some areas and very local polls for neighbourhood committees with control over large budgets have achieved high turnouts.

These changes in method do not solve the underlying problems of democracy. As ever, the scarce resource is time and with it understanding. But they are steps towards more direct engagement by the public in the decisions made on their behalf.

Multiple levels

The fourth principle is the potential to see every issue, every task through many frames from the neighbourhood to the global. Governance now takes place at multiple levels – local, regional, national, European, global – between which there are few clear boundaries. Local phenomena, like asylum or drugs, or the pressures on the education system, cannot be understood or addressed in isolation from global events. Policy increasingly straddles old divides. The ugly word 'intermestic' describes how issues like energy security, cybercrime or migration cut across older definitions of foreign affairs.

At the same time one of the great achievements of the information society has been the rapid emergence of something akin to a global demos. Global public opinion has made itself felt around Kyoto, Afghanistan, debt cancellation and Africa. It makes its strength felt in the actions to tackle conflict, in humanitarian responses to disaster, in the outlawing of genocide, and in the way that some of the 'memes' of democracy, social justice and human rights have spread faster than trade or foreign direct investment in the last decade.

Yet the global demos poses acute problems. No one has designed even in theory a way for people to sense sovereignty in exercising power along with 6 billion others. Some bodies operate on the principle of one nation one vote, some one dollar one vote, and some are effectively weighted by military power – while oddly no international institution works on the principle of one citizen one vote. In a world of imbalanced power this may be inevitable, but it is in tension with the promise of distributed control.

I doubt that we will see the emergence of nation-state type forms at the global level: parliaments, armies, currencies. More likely is a much more complex system of parallel agencies, variable geometry alliances and difficult models of accountability, in all of which the informal aspects are as important as the formal ones. A good example of this is the online network of legislatures being promoted by Earth Action, bringing together 25,000 legislators representing 60 per cent of the world's population with the potential to organise discussion groups over everything from stem cell regulation to terrorism. This will have no formal power but potentially could have a great deal of influence.

Leanness

The fifth principle is leanness. The first wave of productivity gains from information technology were exploited in manufacturing. Only belatedly did private services experience major gains. Now public sectors stand to gain even more than the private sector because so much of what they do involves the collection, processing and dissemination of information and knowledge; these lie at the very heart of government. Yet the realisation of these gains depends on radical reform of processes, structures and rules.

Conclusion

Seeing the connectedness of things is the starting point for understanding a world that otherwise appears baffling. Economics, environment and security do not exist in neatly demarcated boxes. Nor do nations, companies or even families. Yet it is far easier to assume a world without connections, a world of fewer dimensions where simpler heuristics carry us through. This is perhaps the hardest aspect of a connected world and the reason why our concepts and institutions may be doomed to lag behind the reality they seek to make sense of.

Geoff Mulgan is Head of Policy in the Office of Prime Minister Tony Blair, but writes here in a personal capacity.

Notes

1   G Mulgan, *Connexity: responsibility, freedom, business and power in the new century* (London: Vintage, 1998).
2   G Mulgan, *Communication and Control: networks and the new economies of communication* (Cambridge: Polity Press, 1991).

Editors' note

A significant feature of the changing landscape of educational reform in the UK and beyond is the increasing emphasis on collaboration and networking. This shift challenges the dominance of the standards agenda and the competitive ethic that has defined educational policy since the 1980s. Networking between schools is increasingly recognised as a key driver of school improvement in so far as it encourages professional collaboration, innovation, the spread of good practice, and the strengthening of mutual accountability and transparency across groups of schools and 'communities' of practitioners.

To help us understand the nature of this shift and what it means for the future of educational reform, we asked leading thinkers on both sides of the Atlantic to give us their perspective. In chapter 5 distinguished US academics Ann Lieberman and Diane Wood provide some important insights into networks and teacher learning gleaned from the National Writing Project. Demos Associate and leading UK education thinker David Hargreaves then responds to their essay and offers some broader reflections on disciplined innovation within educational networks in chapter 6.

Networks – these loose and flexible organisational forms – are becoming an important way to organise teachers and schools . . .

Untangling the threads

Ann Lieberman
Diane Wood

DEM☺S

5. Untangling the threads

networks, community and teacher learning in the National Writing Project

Ann Lieberman and Diane Wood

In the press for higher standards on the one hand and test results on the other, much of what we are learning about the necessity and support for teacher learning in professional communities is getting lost. Questions about how teachers learn, what they do with what they learn, and whether it ever shows up in what students accomplish are all being buried. But these are precisely the kinds of questions that might lead us to understand better how to build an essential bridge between teachers' professional development and student learning.

It was these questions that excited us, serving as an impetus for a 1998–2000 study of two sites of the National Writing Project (NWP),[1] arguably the single most successful professional development network in the United States. We wanted to find out what teachers learned in the NWP; what, if anything, they took back to their classrooms; and how it showed up in the work they did with students.[2] Although we already understood that the sites were organised locally and yet were linked nationally, we wanted to know more about how these organisational arrangements were developed and sustained and what effects such arrangements had on teacher learning.

In the beginning

Long before we began our study we had heard from teachers that the NWP 'transformed' their lives. We wanted to know exactly what they meant by that. How, from the perspective of teachers, could a professional development project be called transformative? We were particularly interested in this question because, when most teachers talked to us about professional development, they described it as a waste of time and an interruption to their work rather than a support for it. Typical in-services, they often complained, rarely provide follow-up and, even when a topic is interesting, it rarely has anything to do with helping them in their classrooms. What was it, we wondered, about the NWP that seemed to earn such passionate accolades from teachers?

We began our study aware that networks – these seemingly loose and flexible organisational forms – are becoming an important way to organise teachers and schools in productive efforts toward school improvement.[3] We also recognised there are growing and deepening understandings about the power of professional communities for teacher learning, though such communities are complicated, rare and fragile.[4] A crucial question left hanging, however, is whether or not network learning ever actually finds its way into classroom teaching and student accomplishment.

We learned that the NWP is a national network made up of many local networks throughout the country. Each local site comprises a school–university partnership offering summer and year-long professional development for teachers. The NWP bills itself as a professional development initiative, providing multiple avenues for teachers to learn about literacy and writing. Because the NWP has been around since 1974 we had met many NWP teachers over the years and knew how ardently they affiliated themselves with their professional community and its mission. Research literature exists, of course, about networks, about professional communities, and about teacher learning. But the NWP had integrated all of these so completely and placed them in such synergistic relationship with one another that to study the dynamics of this interplay offers a particularly intriguing, yet daunting challenge. The more we became immersed in our study, the more we struggled to untangle these tightly woven threads in order to understand what was going on.

Given the complexities, we decided to begin by studying two sites that are, according to the national directors, particularly well functioning. Both we and the directors wanted the study to focus on sites that negotiated different geographical regions and socio-economic conditions. We settled on the site centred at University of California at Los Angeles (UCLA), a decidedly urban setting, and one centred at Oklahoma State University (OSU) in Stillwater, Oklahoma, a site encompassing a mid-size city, small towns and rural areas. By closely observing activities in both sites and interviewing directors and participating teachers, we gleaned some important understanding about the longevity and success of this professional development initiative.

The five-week invitational institute

We were told by the NWP leadership, both national and site directors, that we needed to attend and make sense of the five-week summer invitational, the initiating experience for new NWP teachers, because there lay 'the heart of the writing project'. After we had seen the institutes first-hand at both UCLA and OSU, we recognised that a seamless set of activities unfolding over the five weeks succeeded in galvanising a professional community. The 'model', as everyone called it, has three interrelated features:

O   creating forms for teachers to teach one another their best
     practices
O   providing opportunities for teachers to write and share in
     response groups
O   engaging teachers in reading and discussing relevant
     literature and research.

These seemingly straightforward ideas provide the frame for the five-week institutes. As teachers teach and learn from one another's practice, write and share their writing, and read and discuss research, they rotate through a series of roles. For examples, they become their colleagues' teachers when giving teaching demonstrations or providing helpful feedback on colleagues' teaching and writing. By turns, they also become learners as they play audience to presentations, get feedback after sitting in the 'author's chair', and engage in research and professional discussions. By rotating such jobs as logging the days' activities and bringing in food for snacks, they play the role of nurturing and responsible colleagues, attentive to the needs of a developing professional community.

Subtly underpinning these activities are the habits of mind necessary for the process of good writing. Teachers learn to reflect on their own intentions as human beings and professionals and choose compelling topics to pursue. They have the space and time for pre-writing reflection, for drafting and getting feedback, for editing and revising. They learn how their writing changes depending on their purposes and intended audiences.

These activities, done in community, help teachers make important connections. Teaching, like writing, requires clear and compelling purpose, trials and errors, and revisions. And, like writing, it flourishes best when taken public for collegial edification and critique. Moreover, writing and teaching are both bolstered by reading and research. Teachers who teach writing effectively and comprehensively have more to do than simply teach the process. They also draw on composition theory and cover such topics as genre, style, grammar, structure, voice, audience and rhetoric. Over the five weeks, an institute curriculum takes shape, incorporating both the active process of writing and salient topics in literacy education. Moreover, the curriculum makes clear connections to local educational challenges. But it was initially honouring teachers' knowledge that engages teachers and encourages them to hold up their teaching for feedback and critique.

Many sites (ours included) ask teachers to write three pieces: an autobiographical re-creation of an experience; a personal essay inspired by an experience; and an experimental piece – a poem, story, or one-act play. For a concluding assignment, teachers are asked to address an issue on the teaching of writing or to write a journal article for submission or a policy statement for their school. In this way teachers experience what it means to be a student and they feel viscerally what it means to engage in writing.

By the second day of the institute, teachers are reading their unfinished pieces, working in their writing groups, teaching lessons to a large group, reading educational literature and participating in discussion groups. As the weeks progress, the institute runs itself as the teachers take over primary responsibility for its rich, varied and intense curriculum. Out of the give and take of these learning activities, institute fellows develop characteristic ways of interacting with one another. They develop, in effect, social practices that weave together the process and content of their learning and embed the cultural expectations and norms of the NWP, creating a strong professional community. By the end of the institute, fellows have internalised these practices, which include:

- O approaching every colleague as a potentially valuable contributor
- O encouraging teachers to teach other teachers
- O creating public forums for sharing, dialogue, and critique
- O turning ownership of learning over to learners
- O situating learning in practice and relationships as well as relevant knowledge
- O providing multiple entry points into learning communities
- O thinking about teaching through reflection on learning
- O sharing leadership
- O adopting an enquiry stance
- O and rethinking professional identity and linking it to the professional community.

The writing project approach to developing good writers and good teachers underscores two principles. First, *deep understanding arises from practice* – in both of its common meanings. That is, both writers and teachers learn from doing. Writers get better at writing by actually writing and teachers get better by teaching. Moreover, both improve by practising in public. Valuing knowledge grounded in practice gives rise to the second principle: *teachers are the best teachers of other teachers*. Those actually involved in practice gain contextualised understandings that make their ideas especially compelling and believable. By taking the position that those who practise writing or teaching are most likely to be good at teaching it, the NWP foregrounds expertise rooted in practice and elevates the peer-to-peer approach to learning rather than the expert to novice approach.

Developing a local network

As we observed both of these institutes, we saw the seeds of a network sown. The institutes induct teachers into a learning community where they can concentrate on their own individual learning and yet grow from the learning agendas of others. While providing opportunities for teachers to discover and nurture a potential talent – teaching other teachers what they have learned from practice – the institutes lay the fundamental basis for the network. Having seen the worth of teachers learning from one another, many fellows leave the institutes committed to the professional development of their teaching colleagues. At UCLA, for instance, there are over 40 teacher consultants (TCs) who now run professional development programmes throughout LA county.

Many of the active TCs with whom we talked told us that, when they taught other teachers, they continued to learn themselves. For instance, a number of teachers found that in sharing their teaching practices with their fellow teachers, they became quite articulate about the *hows* and *whys*. Despite having built expertise over the years as they tried, honed and shaped these practices, teaching them to other teachers always provided fresh insights and deeper understandings.

Although many of those teachers who successfully complete the institutes become TCs, there are some who choose not to participate in teaching other teachers. Those who do, however, are frequently kept quite busy providing professional development for schools and districts, and they get paid for their work. Some get involved in special interest groups on topics of particular concern, such as writing in bilingual classrooms or improving advanced placement teaching. Others lead or participate in teacher research groups that meet throughout the year. Figures indicate that a substantial leadership cadre develops in each site and that the experience is powerful.[5] As one teacher consultant explained:

> On one level TCs work a lot on their own teaching. The continued discussions with teachers about teaching, whether giving a presentation or at meetings regarding new NWP projects...On another level, you learn a lot about teacher learning through experience. It is not explicit...you have to stretch your thinking as a presenter as to what texts and structures you can use to give your audience a chance to experience the presentation rather than to watch it.

Moreover, the NWP itself provides opportunities for leadership in the organisation. At each local site an advisory board of TCs is created ensuring that the local site stays rooted in teachers' definitions of their classroom needs. The UCLA site leadership consists of a director, co-director, three associate directors (all teachers) and others in the university who works with schools. Similarly at OSU, several teacher consultants help create the policies for a year-long programme as they gain experience and provide an important voice in the development of the local network.

Summer and year-long programmes

Although all sites hold a summer invitational institute in common, the types of formats they develop and the content of their professional development differ in interesting ways. The particulars of the context place demands on the networks as they respond to state and local policies as well as to differences in urban, rural and suburban environments. The social practices learned in the summer invitational enact and flesh out core values in the sites, allowing managers to make the necessary adaptations to their contexts without losing the core of what it means to be a NWP site. For example, at UCLA, a 24-year-old site, two state-wide initiatives have greatly affected teaching and learning in the Los Angeles district. Proposition 227 limits a bilingual student to one year of English immersion, and high stakes standardised tests are used as the criteria for passing and failing courses and graduating from high school. Summer offerings of the UCLA site respond to such changing policy contexts for teachers. The UCLA site, in response to Proposition 227 and high stakes testing, organised summer workshops, such as 'Writing from Day One', a week-long offering to help teachers with strategies that enable bilingual students to improve their writing while they are learning English. 'Research to Reading', a state-wide programme, became another offering, this one designed to help teachers avoid narrowing the literacy curriculum by demonstrating that serious incorporation of language arts standards could ultimately lead to higher test scores and to better writing.

At OSU, because the site encompasses such large distances, housing arrangements are made for the five-week invitational. Whenever possible, workshops are arranged to piggy-back on other occasions and minimise the driving time for teachers. To provide a measure of consistency the OSU site has created its own model of writing project work, designed to reach out to teachers in remote towns and rural areas and to bring new and experienced teachers the benefits of teaching demonstrations, opportunities for teacher writing, writing groups and teacher research.

These examples speak to ways that teachers can contribute to the learning of colleagues while continuing their own learning. They also speak to the flexibility and adaptability that a network-like way of organising affords. The NWP's network structure keeps it sensitive to a dynamic and changing environment, while its social practices keep its cultural identity intact and sustain its broader mission.

Besides responding to local needs, the NWP has further ways to answer the professional development needs of teachers. The national office, for instance, helps facilitate sub-networks that cut across sites.

These networks work on common problems identified by the TCs and brought to the attention of the national office. To date, the NWP has four such sub-networks: Project Outreach (formed when the NWP realised that it was not serving poor and minority populations equitably); the Urban Sites (which works through particular problems of language and low-achieving schools); Rural Sites (a network focusing on rural needs with a particular focus on technology); and the English as a Second Language network (focusing on second language learners). The national office coordinates the evaluation and documentation of all 167 sites, its quarterly and bimonthly publications and, increasingly, books written by and about the writing project.

Teacher learning in the National Writing Project

Also enmeshed in each summer institute (and the forthcoming workshops facilitated by TCs) is a view of learning that turns conventional professional development on its head. Instead of teaching teachers someone else's ideas of how they should improve their teaching, the institute begins with *what teachers know* and then moves to what others have learned. This respect for teacher knowledge is so powerful that teachers eventually open themselves up to going public with their writing and teaching – in an environment that invites feedback and critique. It is not hard to see over time how teachers learn from one another, constantly thinking about how particular strategies can be adapted to suit their particular students.

Besides learning from one another, teachers are introduced to a wide variety of reading materials including books to expand their own classroom library. They learn by reading and discussing research on literacy and by being taught by experienced TCs who have become expert in particular areas (such as assessment and multicultural literature). In turn, teachers, through the process of being in a new group, learn how to become good community members (for instance, sharing the responsibility for being a presenter on one day and an audience the next, or being the 'logger' of the day's events). Teacher learning here becomes multifaceted. Teachers are learning by presenting their own practice, by listening to others, by reading and discussing research and literature together, by being in a group, by taking responsibility for the groups' needs, and by taking risks together. In short, they are learning how to be members of a democratic community that values them, their knowledge and their continued growth.

In this article we have discussed the site as a local network embedded in a national network bringing its group of teachers into a professional community that respects the variety of ways that teachers learn. But the magic of the writing project is that all these things are tightly integrated into an experience that socialises teachers into a new way of thinking about themselves as teachers. While the social practices provide the core, the network-like way of organising helps develop a local constituency. Untangling these threads has helped us to see a powerful model for professional development and yet another way to develop a professional community situated in teachers' practice.

Ann Lieberman is an emeritus professor at Teachers College, Columbia University, and a senior scholar at the Carnegie Foundation for the Advancement of Teaching. Diane R Wood is an assistant professor in the Educational Leadership Program, College of Education and Human Development, University of Southern Maine. This essay is an edited version of an article that first appeared as 'Untangling the threads: networks, community and teacher learning in the National Writing Project', Teachers and Teaching 8, no 3–4 (2002), pp 295–302.

Notes

1   A site in the NWP grows out of a university–school partnership. The university is the 'owner' of the site. Beginning sites receive $20,000 and must document their plans and their work and keep accurate information about who participates and the nature of their formats for work during the year. The programme is sponsored by the federal government.

2   This paper quotes liberally from A Lieberman and D Wood, *Inside the National Writing Project: network learning and classroom teaching – a new synthesis* (New York: Teacher College Press, 2003).

3   J Adams, *Taking Charge of Curriculum: teacher networks and curriculum*

implementation (New York: Teachers College Press, 2000); A Lieberman and MW McLaughlin, 'Networks for educational change: powerful and problematic', in *Phi Delta Kappan* 73, no 9 (1992); A Lieberman and M Grolnick, 'Networks and reform in American education', *Teachers College Record* 98, no 1 (1996).

4   P Grossman and S Wineburg (forthcoming), 'In pursuit of community', *Teachers College Record*; MW McLaughlin and J Talbert, *Professional Communities and the Work of High School Teaching* (Chicago: University of Chicago Press, 2001); E Wenger, *Communities of Practice: learning, meaning, and identity* (Cambridge: Cambridge University Press, 2000); J Westheimer, *Among Schoolteachers: community, autonomy and ideology in teacher's work* (New York: Teachers College Press, 1998).

5   M St John et al with assistance from A Murphy, *The National Writing Project: client satisfaction and program impact* (Inverness, Ca: Inverness Research Associates, 2001).

Innovation is a social, interactive process rather than one of individual creativity, and networks play a vital role . . .

Networks, knowledge and innovation

David H Hargreaves

DEM⊙S

6. Networks, knowledge and innovation
reflections on teacher learning

David H Hargreaves

A response to the previous chapter, 'Untangling the threads', by Ann Lieberman and Diane Wood.

Academic educationists, like teachers in schools, have strongly held values. Naturally they choose to study phenomena that relate to those values and preferably support them. Ann Lieberman has a distinguished reputation for her work on teachers. I count myself among those influenced by her edited collection of essays, *Building a Professional Culture in Schools* and her book *Teachers – Their World and their Work*.[1] I imagine that she was thrilled to discover what was happening in the National Writing Project, for this is what appears to be a resounding success story about her passion for professional learning among teachers. Her essay, with Diane Wood, glows with the excitement and enthusiasm experienced by educationists who discover some evidence that supports their beliefs and that is welcome 'good news' to a profession longing to have its own beliefs and commitments validated, especially when these collide with government-led initiatives driven by the 'standards agenda'.

In this short response to their essay, which in many ways inspires me as much as it does them, I want to set their ideas and findings in a wider conceptual framework and a rather more sceptical perspective on the achievements of the National Writing Project (NWP). In both ways I seek to contribute to the advancement of academic theory and research, as well as to teacher practices, in a field where rapid change and development can surely be expected.

Professional development and student learning

Lieberman and Wood seek to 'untangle the threads' of the dynamics of the NWP that, in their view, potentially builds the essential bridge between teachers' professional learning (their own passion) and student learning (and its outcomes in measured achievements, the passion of politicians pressing for higher standards). If a *causal* link can be demonstrated between the kinds of teacher practices developed in the NWP and improved student learning, then this not merely adds to our knowledge of 'what works' in schooling; it also validates the approaches to professional learning that Lieberman has long advocated rather than the top-down interventions that have been attractive to political reformers. Lieberman and Wood do not adduce evidence for this causal link: they assume it. If it does exist – and we must look elsewhere for the hard evidence – then the relationship between teachers' professional development and student test scores will, as they claim, be a complex one, with many threads that need to be untangled. Or, to put the matter in more conventional research terms, there will be many variables involved and these are likely to interact with one another in complex ways.

In essence, the essay offers a list of possible variables, but little insight into which of them might be of particular importance or into the ways in which they interact (or, in their terms, become 'tightly woven'). The evidence is based on interviews with the participants and observation of some (unspecified) activities. It appears that the participants were enthusiasts for the project and their claims of its success are taken at face value. It is not clear how much of the analysis is based on the accounts yielded by the interviews and how much on what is inferred from researchers' observations. It is, in short, a piece of preliminary or exploratory 'soft' research, but the findings are not then set within a harder framework, such as a set of hypotheses that might be tested. This is a pity, for if there is firm evidence of a causal link between certain approaches to teachers' professional development and student achievement, then, as is implicitly suggested, this may extend beyond student writing and apply to a far wider range of teacher practices in classrooms. It could potentially entail the discovery of what has hitherto been elusive: teacher-friendly ways to engage with professional development resulting in improved student outcomes, to the delight of politicians demanding higher standards.

The reluctance to formulate any hypotheses is thus a surprise as well as a pity, for 15 years ago Lieberman presciently understood the need for some hard analysis:

> We often think of solving problems in our own institutions. We rarely think of forming coalitions or networks outside existing formal channels. And it is even rarer that we think of loose, informal collections of people (networks) as catalysts for change. We may very well be in a period where we grossly underestimate both the attack on teachers and the amount of support needed to make improvements in practice... Our concern is understanding [networks] from the inside, getting a sense of the subtleties, and using examples as a way of conceptualising what we know about networks.[2]

At that time, the key ingredients of a successful network, derived from their analysis of educational networks then in existence, were:

O organising for participation
O developmental substance or some agreed content
O developmental mechanism for network interaction and sharing
O planning new rewards, including experimenting with new ideas
O problem-solving orientation to help participants find their own solutions to problems
O diagnosis of what participants know and need

○ strategy-building through action plans
○ organising for linkage among participants with different perspectives and potential contributions.

There appears to be some overlap between 'these eight processes that we consider essential for the creation of a network' and the key ingredients of the NWP, but there are also real differences. The NWP study emphasises, among other factors:

○ teachers teaching professional colleagues about their best practices
○ teachers honouring and respecting the knowledge of colleagues
○ teachers writing as well as meeting and talking
○ teachers getting feedback on their learning and actions
○ teachers rotating through a variety of roles.

How are these differences to be explained? This takes us back to the need to determine the strength of the evidence for NWP, since in their turn the 1990 networks were largely assumed to be successful. Is NWP demonstrably more successful than its predecessors and thus a more reliable source of sound evidence of what makes for success? Does the current evidence on NWP replace the 'key ingredients' suggested in 1992? If our knowledge about networks is accumulating, can we now with confidence proclaim what works and what does not?

Understanding networks

Over the intervening 10 to 15 years, interest in networking, as well as its associated literature, has grown dramatically, but this is not well reflected in the Lieberman and Wood report. Today we have a better grasp of the issues of both the *structure* and *culture* of networks. Networks have many different kinds of structure. Does the NWP have a distinctive structure that differs from those studied in 1990? Indeed, exactly what kind of structure does NWP have? We are told that the networks are organised locally but linked nationally. What are the local networks like? Do they vary much in structure, for example those in the urban rather than rural sites? What are the units of the networks? Are they networks of individual teachers? Or are they sometimes networks of schools? Or could they be both? Does it matter that NWP is in some ways a network of networks? Do networks of networks function differently from networks of institutions (schools) or individuals (teachers)? Are some network structures more successful than others in their impact on student learning? While NWP may be rated an overall success, it seems likely that some sub-networks in some areas will be more successful than others. What are the characteristics of the most and least successful networks? Does this help us to understand the nature of the most important variables in systems of professional networking? Does the teacher consultant act as a kind of hub that helps the network to flourish? Are networks without hubs of some kind more liable to failure or disintegration? What is the role of weak ties in a national network as opposed to what are probably the stronger ties of a local network? In short, is the structure of a network critical to the way it works and influences teacher development and student learning?

While it is difficult to glimpse the structure of the networks from the Lieberman and Wood description, their culture is more visible. Back in 1990 there was relatively little work on social capital, and virtually none in education. Today it is a highly developed – even overdeveloped – concept, not least in the field of networks. For networks have a structural side, the nature of the links between the nodes, but also a cultural aspect, which is usually encapsulated in the term *trust*. The glue behind the strong ties of local networks is trust: without trust, networks rarely prosper. It is possible to argue from the Lieberman and Wood account of the way the NWP was organised and functioned that high levels of social capital were built up among the participants and crucial to the project's success was this generation of high levels of trust between teachers. For example, getting teachers to show their writing to fellow teachers and obtaining feedback on it depends on there being a level of initial trust; if the experience is then felt to be professionally rewarding, it will generate more trust, which in turn strengthens the network itself. It is arguable that NWP succeeded because it tapped and refreshed professional trust among the participating teachers.

To say this is not simply to play with words for, if this hypothesis is correct, there may well be many different ways of generating high levels of social capital in addition to those specified in the analysis of NWP. The explanation may not lie in particular practices, such as teachers engaging in writing, but in the fact that here is one activity that in this particular context helped to generate high social capital. In a different context – another curriculum subject or another aspect of schooling – very different practices may be successful in generating the high social capital that allows teachers to learn with and from their colleagues in a way that benefits their classroom practices. Indeed, one of the things we really do need to untangle is whether peer-to-peer approaches are always better than expert-to-novice ones in education, or whether the latter have often been less successful because they have lacked a basis of social capital. Indeed, expert-to-novice systems do seem to work in apprenticeship-type relationships where trust is well established, as documented by Jean Lave and Etienne Wenger among others.[3] The problem may be not that expert-to-novice approaches are ineluctably destined to failure in the case of teachers' professional learning, but that we have missed out of our analysis the key underlying feature, social capital, and mistakenly assumed that the surface features, the participants' identities as experts and novices, are the critical variables that explain the low success rate.

Networks, knowledge management and innovation

This brings us to another aspect of the wider conceptual framework for networks since 1990, namely the dramatic growth of interest in knowledge management and innovation.

From a knowledge management perspective, what we have traditionally called professional learning is very often a form of knowledge creation and knowledge transfer, alternatively conceived as innovation and the dissemination of such innovation. We now understand better than ever that innovation is very often a social, interactive process rather than one of individual creativity, and that networks play a vital role in the creation and the transfer of new knowledge and innovation. In NWP teachers 'share best practices' and do so in a way that seeks to improve on them as well as spread them. The question thus arises: to what degree would it be advantageous to set the Lieberman and Wood analysis not only in its traditional location of *professional learning* but also in new locations of *knowledge management* and *innovation*? There are at least two advantages of so doing. First, it offers the analysis a new and potentially richer set of concepts in which to set NWP and the analytic frame adopted. Second, it would bring into view a new and different research base.

Best practice

Three examples might help here. Lieberman and Wood commend the ways teachers share their best practices, but they treat the concept of best practice as entirely unproblematic. Exactly what are the defining characteristics of a 'good practice' in NWP? It might, of course, mean nothing more than an ideologically approved or politically correct pedagogical practice within the values of NWP. It might mean a practice that an individual teacher has found to be effective in her private experience and judgement. It might mean one that is demonstrably more effective in ensuring student learning. If NWP is effective in knowledge transfer through its networks, it is rather important that the good practices disseminated are ones that are indeed demonstrably effective by some objective evidence. What action was taken to ascertain the basis of the good practices involved in NWP? How much of this learning could be used in other forms of professional development?

'Good practice' and 'best practice' are often treated as synonyms, even though best is not the same as good. A practice could be considered 'best' if it has been shown to be better – more effective or efficient – than other practices. Did NWP uncover or elaborate on a process of moving from 'good practice', however defined, to a demonstrable 'best practice', rigorously defined? If so, this process would have relevance to a wide range of professional development and reform activities in education.

The process of transfering knowledge

We know that transferring knowledge from one person or one context to another is often difficult, and especially so, as in the case of many of the classroom practices of teachers, when the knowledge involved is heavily tacit rather than explicit, and not easily put into words. It is possible that NWP owed much of its success to the fact that unusual amounts of knowledge were successfully transferred between teachers, which would be rewarding to both donors and recipients of such knowledge. But what exactly were the processes by which the knowledge was transferred and what role did particular forms of networking play in this? The knowledge management literature would entail treating knowledge transfer between teachers as a topic worthy of detailed investigation.

Networks, ICTs and best practice

A third example is the new information and communication technologies (ICTs), which again have grown dramatically over the last decade. We do not know what role the ICTs might play in creating and sustaining professional networks: they will have limits and will have yet to be discovered strengths, even though it is virtually certain that they will complement face-to-face interactions rather than displacing them. ICTs may be of particular importance for networking by teachers who are isolated in their teaching specialism or in their physical location.

At the same time, we should not underestimate the capacity of innovation and best practice networks to devise solutions to problems that arise and to borrow ideas from the internet. Take the way Amazon.com works, for instance. You look up a topic, and are provided with a list of books. You look up a book and in addition to details of its content, price and so on, two further resources are put at your disposal. First, you are offered reviews of the books, by the author or professional reviewers, as well as other Amazon customers. You are also told whether customers found these reviews helpful. Second, Amazon tells you which other books a purchaser of the target book has also bought. Displayed before you is an elaborate set of factual information and evaluations to help you make a more informed decision about book-buying.

Epinions.com offers a similar service. It will search millions of products and services – such as books, movies, cars, restaurants, computers, sports and travel – and tell you where to obtain the lowest price for them and which stores are most trusted by customers. Products and services are reviewed and rated by customers, and these are available to all other customers. Customers rate reviewers for the quality of their reviews, and reviewers whose judgements are trusted by their peers are designated top reviewers. You are also told which other reviewers the top reviewers most trust. You become a top reviewer only if you have earned such a reputation for your advice to other customers.

An innovation and best practice network for teachers might have a similar infrastructure. The quality of an innovation and validity of a claim to good or best practice could be rated by those who had tried to transfer it, as well as by 'experts' such as researchers or Ofsted. Indeed, the trustworthiness of the judges would also be rated by practitioners, for this would be particularly important in relation to judgements or claims about high leverage and ease of transferability. For academic researchers to have to earn their reputation for trustworthiness would be a gain for both them and for teachers. The system would also need to give information on the location of the nearest helper-practitioner or consultant, since accessibility and opportunities for a face-to-face meeting as well as coaching and mentoring are vital. The NWP might be the kind of project to gain from such a development borrowed from ICT in the business world.

Conclusion

Ann Lieberman has been at the forefront of developments in teachers' professional learning and its associated communities and networks. Today understanding the dynamics involved is more important than ever. If we are challenged by more demanding questions, this is because there are more opportunities both for imaginative innovation and for better methods of investigating and analysing these creative developments.

David H Hargreaves is a fellow of Wolfson College, Cambridge, and Chairman of the British Educational Communications and Technology Agency (BECTA). He is a senior associate of Demos and Associate Director (Development and Research) of the Specialist Schools Trust, and was formerly Chief Inspector of the Inner London Education Authority and Chief Executive of the Qualifications and Curriculum Authority. His latest publication is Education Epidemic: transforming secondary schools through innovation networks, *published by Demos in 2003.*

Notes

1   A Lieberman (ed.), *Building a Professional Culture in Schools* (New York: Teachers College Press, 1988); A Lieberman and L Miller, *Teachers – their World and their Work: implications for school improvement* (New York: Teachers College Press, 1992).
2   Lieberman and Miller, *Teachers – their World and their Work*.
3   For example J Lave and E Wenger, *Situated Learning: legitimate peripheral participation* (Cambridge: Cambridge University Press, 1991).

Asked about leadership, most people reach for the organogram. But when it comes to networks there are no such easy answers . . .

Leading between

Paul Skidmore

DEM⊙S

7. Leading between
leadership and trust in a network society

Paul Skidmore

The institutional landscape of modern society is being ripped up. Be they companies or public agencies, individual organisations are finding that the only way to satisfy the changing demands and expectations of customers and citizens is to be embedded in networks of organisations able to stitch together different products, services, resources and skills in flexible combinations and deliver them when and where they are most needed. Splendid isolation is out. Collaboration is in.

But this radical disruption also spells trouble for many of the assumptions we have about what leadership means, what it is for and where we might look for it. Networks challenge our conceptions of leadership, which too often are still rooted in an outmoded 'great man' theory that mistakes the formal authority of status, rank or station with the exercise of leadership. When you ask people about the leadership of an organisation, most people reach for the organogram and point to the top. When it comes to leading across networks there are no such easy answers.

New network-based ways of organising social and economic activity will only thrive if we can evolve new models of leadership that embrace the distinctive 'organising logic' of networks, and do not seek to apply an old set of principles in an environment that has been dramatically altered. We must learn what it means to lead effectively not just within individual organisations, but across the networks of which they are part. 'Leading between' will be the new leadership imperative of the coming decades.

The challenge of leadership in a network society

Our increasing personal and institutional interconnectedness, the long-term trends driving it, and the challenges that arise from it, are all familiar terrain.[1] The organisational responses to these developments have also been chronicled. Companies have been reorganised internally as networks of sub-units, and externally as specialised hubs in distributed production networks involving other suppliers and subcontractors, often crossing national boundaries.[2] This model is exemplified by Cisco Systems, a company that mediates between customers and a diverse array of manufacturers of components used in information technology networks.

According to Shoshana Zuboff and James Maxmin, these trends are set to accelerate and intensify in the coming decades with the emergence of the 'support economy'. Their thesis is that the drive to specialisation has left individual corporations unable to provide the 'deep support' that consumers need to help them navigate through ever-more complex arrays of choice and offering, or to engage with the personals needs and aspirations of individual customers. As a result, most will therefore find themselves drawn into 'federated support networks': fluid configurations of firms brought together to provide unique aggregations of products and services.[3]

The same drive to integrate has also been felt across the public sector. Public policy problems are now understood to cut across traditional institutional boundaries. As Prime Minister Tony Blair put it, 'Even the basic policies, targeted at unemployment, poor skills, low incomes, poor housing, high crime, bad health and family breakdown, will not deliver their full effect unless they are properly linked together. Joined-up problems need joined-up solutions.' Public services are under growing pressure to offer genuinely 'personalised' solutions if they are to meet the individual needs of an increasingly demanding citizenry.[4] Yet the agencies charged with meeting these challenges have spent the last century retreating into ever-more specialised functional silos, supported by powerful institutional, professional and disciplinary cultures or 'tribes' that make effective coordination very difficult.

The trouble is that this increasing interconnectedness does not reduce our requirement for leadership. By creating new and tough problems, and undermining the legitimacy and effectiveness of some of the traditional institutional responses to them, it actively increases it. But the question is what kind of leadership do we need?

Old theories die hard

Too often in the face of these pressures we look to locate leadership at the top of institutions. In an uncertain world, we expect individual leaders to somehow provide certainty where previous leaders could not: 'We call for someone with answers, decision, strength, and a map of the future, someone who knows where we ought to be going – someone in short who can make hard problems simple.'[5]

In education, for example, we have seen the rise of 'superheads' – headteachers and principals brought into failing schools and given more resources and higher remuneration on the assumption that they will personally be able to reverse the decline, often with very mixed results.

In local government we have seen the introduction of US-style elected mayors, in the hope that concentrating power in a single office will create more visible and effective leadership. But so far these have failed to capture the imagination or energise citizens, and in the few municipalities that have opted for local mayors electoral turnouts have not markedly improved.

In business we have seen the 'cult of the CEO', with senior executives paid vast salaries because corporate survival is seen to depend on attracting and retaining talent. But as the controversy over 'rewards for failure' indicates, many such remuneration packages are only tenuously linked to actual business performance, and in a number of notorious cases (for example, at GE Marconi) executives have been given multi-million pound severance packages even after leading their companies to the verge of ruin.

Finally, in the reform agenda of the European Union, particularly as embodied in the recent Constitutional Convention, we are seeing a push towards a conventionally hierarchical model of political leadership, with greater decision-making power concentrated at the centre. As Mark Leonard has argued, this search for some neat institutional arrangement ignores the fact that the EU is more like a network than a traditional organisation. It misses the chance to breathe new life into a debate hamstrung by the false choice between federal superstate and a free trade area, and could undermine the very flexibility on which EU integration has depended.[6]

What is striking about all these examples is that the response to a crisis of authority is to reinforce the traditional model of leadership. We seek saviours, and then berate them when they fail. Wherever we look, our instinctive response to the complexity of organisational life is to strengthen the very forms of institution, and institutional authority, that it has exhausted. The command-and-control form of authority on which most large organisations were built does not tally with the underlying social reality. It is at odds both with the complexity of the context in which they are asked to operate *and* the prevailing social expectations about how they should behave. 'Control,' as Veenkamp et al argue, 'seems more important but less feasible than ever before.'[7]

We need to take a different starting point.

Leading with questions not answers

In *Leadership Without Easy Answers*, Ronald Heifetz argues that conventional models of leadership confuse it with authority. In so doing, they perpetuate the seductive but dangerous myth that leadership is about influence and persuading people to follow a particular vision. So 'followers' look to a leader to solve their problems for them, ignoring their own capacity (and responsibility) to solve it for themselves. People in authority believe that their vision of change is legitimate simply because they are 'leaders'. And when things go wrong, it is the 'leaders' who are blamed and replaced, with little or no reflection on the underlying causes of the problem.

To put it another way, leadership is not something you are but something you do; it is an activity, not a position. For Heifetz, leadership is about mobilising people to do what he calls *adaptive work*. It is about forcing them to confront the gap between the rhetoric of what they are trying to achieve and the reality of their current capacity to achieve it. Leaders do not try to impose change. Instead they make the case for why change is necessary, and then make the space for it occur. Leaders create a holding environment for those they lead, managing the tension and stress that change inevitably generates but never allowing them to run away from it.

This simple insight is profound in relation to leadership within an organisation, but it is revolutionary in helping us to see the challenge of leadership across networks. Divorced from formal positions of authority, leadership – mobilising people to do adaptive work – is as feasible between organisations as it is within them, even if the resources that are deployed and constraints experienced may vary depending on the context.

The six characteristics of network leadership
So what is it that network leaders do?

Network leaders lead from the outside in
As the Global Business Network notes, many firms think about their strategy from the inside-out, beginning with the organisation's purpose and core strengths, then working out to explore its marketplaces and only then looking externally for broader, underlying shifts that might matter.[8] The problem is that by the time they get there they have imposed so many filters that they're not seeing the real world at all. They are looking through the lens of their own perspectives and assumptions about what matters, not those of the customers, users or citizens they are there to serve.

Network leaders start from the outside-in. They start with the deepest needs of their users, and work back to establish the configuration of organisations, resources and capacities needed to meet them. The task then is to find ways of persuading other organisations of the need to work together.

Network leaders mobilise disparate supplies of energy

Leadership is often seen to be synonymous with decisive action: defining a vision and pursuing it. Network leaders understand that decisive action may be of little use in an unpredictable world, particularly when the knowledge about how best to improve performance often resides in the tacit and explicit knowledge of front-line staff. As Nonaka and Takeuchi argue, finding ways to unlock and harness this knowledge by developing procedures for the creation and sharing of knowledge among staff is therefore a crucial leadership task.[9] In this context, leadership is less about decision than deliberation.

Douglas Rushkoff argues that the real power and attraction of the internet is not the knowledge or facts or ideas it supplies but the opportunity to interact with others: 'Con*tent* is not king. Con*tact* is king.'[10] The same goes for leadership. Network leaders know that they cannot provide some definitive vision statement but they can structure the right kind of conversation. They can create a language that enables people to cross boundaries – within or beyond their organisation – that they otherwise would not.

Network leaders foster trust and empower others to act

But deliberation does not mean inaction. Networked leadership is not leadership by committee, where the sole criterion for action is the lowest common denominator. As Danny Chesterman argues in his study of leadership in local multi-agency partnerships, 'The first assumption is that consensus is necessary by all before any partnership can act collaboratively...We talk as if agreement is a precondition for action. It isn't. But sufficient trust is.'[11] Network leaders understand that different actors will not always agree on the appropriate course of action, not least because in a complex world the correct path will rarely be clear, and stumbling upon it may require processes of trial and error, and learning by doing.

By sharing perspectives and building understanding, however, it is possible to foster the trust and the set of common values on which all networks depend, and which are robust enough to withstand considerable variety in the actions undertaken by others. Geoff Mulgan describes the medals once awarded to the general who disobeyed orders, but in so doing changed the course of battle.[12] It is a spirit that lives on today. The day before the Eden Centre in Cornwall opened to the public, managing director Tim Smit called the staff together and said, 'Tomorrow, people will ask you for things, or to do things, we haven't thought of. If you respond in a way which goes wrong, no one will blame you. If you do nothing, I'll sack you.'[13] 'True authority', as Capra puts it, 'consists in empowering others to act.'[14]

Network leaders help people grow out of their comfort zones

Network leadership would not be necessary if the organisational silos in which many of us find ourselves were not so attractive. As senior managers responsible for multi-professional learning in Britain's NHS explained, these 'tribes' provide us with stability, a sense of identity and a shared language that allows information to travel fast. Above all, they allow us to maintain our existing routines: 'It's very seductive to fall back into old behaviours because that's the known world,' as one put it.[15] In the public sector, multi-agency working is now *de rigueur*, with local service delivery of everything from education (such as Excellence in Cities clusters) to economic development (like local strategic partnerships) structured around networks of agencies. Unfortunately, partnership is often treated as a structure rather than an activity, and formal mechanisms for decision-making are put in place before the different actors have had a chance to move out of their particular silos.[16]

Network leaders understand the attraction of these comfort zones but look for ways to help people grow out of them. Traditional performance management systems typically reward people for staying within particular silos and running away from the problems that fall between the gaps but, as Karen Stephenson shows, developments in social network analysis have allowed a number of organisations to begin to reward people for running *towards* them. In the public sector, extrinsic rewards have often proved effective in the short run, with organisations happy to work in partnership so long as there is a clear and immediate return on their investment. But longer-term commitment seems to reside in more intrinsic rewards: tapping into people's sense of professionalism, and reconnecting them with the higher moral purpose that first motivated them to enter that particular field.

Network leaders are lead learners not all-knowers

Certainty of vision is wrapped up in many of our mental models of leadership. But in the modern world this can be a dangerous myth, leading us down seductive avenues that turn out to be blind alleys – think of Cable and Wireless' doomed foray into business services under Chief Executive Graham Wallace, a strategy that may have seemed sensible at the height of the internet bubble but a few years and £35 billion in lost shareholder value later increasingly looked like a great example of what Michael Fullan calls the 'visions that blind'.[17]

'The original meaning of authority', Fritjof Capra has noted, 'is not "power to command" but a "firm basis for knowing and acting".'[18] Given the complexity of modern organisational life, it seems the only firm basis for acting is to be a permanent learner. Network leaders do not see themselves as all-knowers but as lead learners. They understand that a large part of leadership is about shutting up and listening. Network leaders make a point of not having all the answers.

Network leaders nurture other leaders

At Lipson Community College, a large secondary school in Plymouth, the pool of potential leadership talent is drawn very widely. In fact, it extends to students themselves. Older students have received coaching as mediators to help younger pupils settle disputes or other problems getting in the way of their learning without involving staff. Students of any age are encouraged to become 'lead learners', trained to take real responsibility for their learning and to mentor others.

Candidates for new teaching posts are asked to teach a lesson, and students in the class give feedback on their performance to the school's management team. Smaller groups of students who have been given special training then comprise one of the interview panels and often have the main say in who is appointed. Principal Steve Baker talks of playing a long game through a sustained programme of activities that brings in, reaches out to and raises expectations of the whole community.

Network leaders like these understand that leadership is not about a simple transaction between leaders and led. Instead they reach back to the ancient ideal of *self-government* as the ultimate goal of leadership. They understand that most systems – from organisations to cities to biological ecosystems – are too complex and unpredictable to be controlled from the top-down. Yet they display an underlying tendency towards self-organisation and order, leading to what Briggs calls 'meaningful patterns of uncertainty'.[19] This self-organisation can be shaped in purposeful ways, provided we can develop leadership models that *distribute leadership across organisations* rather than imposing it from the top. To align leadership with the built-in instinctive adaptive responses of organisations, in other words, network leaders understand the need to nurture other leaders wherever they may be found. As Sun Tzu put it long ago: 'The good leader is the one the people adore; the wicked leader is the one the people despise; the great leader is the one the people say "we did it ourselves".'

Trust, betrayal and network leadership

Network leadership is increasingly necessary if organisations are to satisfy the needs of those they serve. But the mental leap involved in accepting network leadership is not easy. Perhaps the most important commodity for this new conception of leadership to take hold is trust. Leaders in hierarchies rely on chains of command and clear lines of accountability to ensure that the 'right' decisions are made, and the 'right' people censured if they fail. Network leadership rejects that model of authority, and the blame games it promotes.

But network leaders nonetheless carry responsibility, in particular to preserve the trust on which their networks depend. In an unpredictable world in which some failures are almost bound to happen, that is a tough challenge. Acknowledging the depth of our interdependence with others, and the limited capacity of our leaders to manage it, will be a frightening experience. It is much more convenient to think that leaders will be saviours – and that we have someone to blame when things do not go our way. But if it wakes us up to the potential within each of us to solve our own problems, then so much the better.

Paul Skidmore is a senior researcher at Demos.

Notes

1   See for example G Mulgan, *Connexity: responsibility, freedom, business and power in the new century* (London: Vintage, 1998).

2   M Castells, *Rise of the Network Society* (Oxford: Blackwell, 1996); A Giddens, *The Third Way: the renewal of social democracy* (Cambridge: Polity Press, 1998).

3   S Zuboff and J Maxmin, *The Support Economy: why corporations are failing individuals and the next stage of capitalism* (London: Allen Lane, 2003).

4   C Leadbeater, T Bentley and J Wilsdon, *The Adaptive State: strategies for personalising the public realm* (London: Demos, 2003).

5   R Heifetz, *Leadership Without Easy Answers* (Cambridge, MA: Belknapp Press, 1994).

6   M Leonard, *Network Europe* (London: Foreign Policy Centre, 1999).

7   T Veenkamp, T Bentley and A Buenfino, *People Flow: managing migration in a New European Commonwealth* (London: Demos, 2003).

8   Global Business Network, *What Next? Exploring the new terrain for business* (Cambridge, MA: Perseus, 2002).

9   I Nonaka and H Takeuchi, *The Knowledge Creating Company* (Oxford: Oxford University Press, 1995).

10 D Rushkoff, *Open Source Democracy* (London: Demos, 2003).

11 D Chesterman with M Horne, *Local Authority?* (London: Demos, 2003).

12 G Mulgan, *Communication and Control: networks and the new economies of communication* (Cambridge: Polity Press, 1991).

13 T Smit, *Eden* (Bantam Books, 2001), cited in J Chapman, *System Failure* (London: Demos, 2002).

14 F Capra, *The Hidden Connections* (London: HarperCollins, 2002).

15   M Horne, P Skidmore and J Holden, *Learning Communities and NHSU* (London: Demos/NHSU, 2004).

16   Chesterman with Horne, *Local Authority?*

17   M Fullan cited in D Wilkinson and E Appelbee, *Implementing Holistic Government* (Bristol: Demos/Policy Press, 1999).

18   Capra, *Hidden Connections.*

19   Cited in Zuboff and Maxmin, *The Support Economy.*

Disparities of wealth appear as a law of economic life that emerges naturally as an organisational feature of a network . . .

The science of inequality

Mark Buchanan

DEM☺S

8. The science of inequality

Mark Buchanan

Historically, economists have been obsessed with arguments over how equitable or inequitable the distribution of wealth is among individuals. This is perhaps the most controversial and inflammatory of all economic topics. As economist John Kenneth Galbraith noted in his history of the field: 'The explanation and rationalization of the resulting inequality has commanded some of the greatest, or in any case some of the most ingenious, talent in the economics profession.'[1]

What is this 'inequality' that Galbraith refers to? We all know, of course, that a few people are very wealthy and that most of us have far less. But the inequality of the distribution of wealth has a surprisingly universal character. You might well expect the distribution to vary widely from country to country, as each nation has its own distinct political organisation and resources – some nations relying on agriculture, others on heavy industry – while their peoples have unique cultural expectations, habits and skills. However, towards the end of the nineteenth century, an Italian engineer-turned-economist named Vilfredo Pareto discovered a pattern in the distribution of wealth that appears to be every bit as universal as the laws of thermodynamics or chemistry.

Suppose that in Britain, China or the United States, or any other country for that matter, you count the number of people worth say, £10,000. Suppose you then count the number worth £20,000, £30,000 and so on, covering many levels of wealth both large and small, and finally plot the results on a graph. You would find, as Pareto did, many individuals at the poorer end of the scale and progressively fewer at the wealthy end. This is hardly surprising. But Pareto discovered that the numbers dwindle in a very special way: towards the wealthy end, each time you double the amount of wealth, the number of people falls by a constant factor.

Big deal? It is. Mathematically, a 'Pareto distribution' of this form has a notable characteristic, as it implies that *a small fraction of the wealthiest people always possesses a lion's share of a country's riches.* It could be the case that the bulk of humanity in the middle of distribution was in possession of most of the wealth. But it isn't so. In the United States something like 80 per cent of the wealth is held by only 20 per cent of the people, and the numbers are similar in Chile, Bolivia, Japan, South Africa or the nations of Western Europe. It might be 10 per cent owning 90 per cent, 5 per cent owning 85 per cent, or 3 per cent owning 96 per cent, but in all cases, wealth seems to migrate naturally into the hands of the few. Indeed, although good data is sadly lacking, studies in the mid-1970s based on interviews with Soviet emigrants even suggested that wealth inequality in the communist Soviet Union was then comparable to that of the UK.[2]

An underlying order?

What causes this striking regularity across nations? Does it simply reflect the natural distribution of human talent? Or, is there some devilish conspiracy among the rich? Not surprisingly, given the strong emotions stirred by matters of wealth and its disparity, economists in the past have, as Galbraith noted, flocked to such questions. Today, these questions again seem quite timely, as, if anything, the degree of inequity seems to be growing.

In the United States, according to economist Paul Krugman:

> *The standard of living of the poorest 10 percent of American families is significantly lower today than it was a generation ago. Families in the middle are, at best, slightly better off. Only the wealthiest 20 percent of Americans have achieved income*

growth anything like the rates nearly everyone experienced between the 1940s and early 1970s. Meanwhile, the income of families high in the distribution has risen dramatically with something like a doubling of real incomes of the top 1 percent.[3]

A similar story could be told for the United Kingdom and many other countries, especially in Eastern Europe, over the past two decades.

Something similar is taking place on the global stage. Globalisation is frequently touted – especially by those with vested economic interests such as multinational corporations and investment banks – as a process that will inevitably help the poor of the world. To be sure, greater technological and economic integration on a global scale certainly ought to have the potential to do so. Yet as Nobel Prize-winning economist and former chief economist of the World Bank Joseph Stiglitz notes in his recent *Globalization and its Discontents*:

A growing divide between the haves and the have-nots has left increasing numbers in the Third World in dire poverty, living on less than a dollar a day. Despite repeated promises of poverty reduction made over the last decade of the twentieth century, the actual number of people living in poverty has actually increased by almost 100 million. This occurred at the same time that total world income actually increased by an average of 2.5 per cent annually.[4]

What is the origin of these distinct but seemingly related trends? Economists can, of course, offer a great many relevant observations. Stiglitz condemns the international economic policies of the Western nations and the International Monetary Fund as reflecting the needs of special financial and commercial interests regardless of the damage inflicted on the developing nations. One can point also to tax cuts for the very wealthy (a general theme of the 1980s and 1990s, especially in the US and UK), to changes in international markets, the influence of new communication technologies and so on. These are all legitimate and insightful points.

But might there be a more general perspective – a general science that would illuminate the basic forces that lead to wealth inequity? Conventional economic theory has never managed to explain the origin of Pareto's universal pattern. Ironically, however, a pair of physicists, venturing across interdisciplinary lines, has recently done so. To understand their thinking, forget for the moment about personal ingenuity, intelligence, entrepreneurial skills and the other factors that might clearly influence an individual's economic destiny. Instead, take one step into the abstract and think of an economy as a network of interacting people and focus on how wealth flows about in this network.

That's the way the money goes

Each of us has a certain amount of wealth and, over the days and weeks, this amount changes in one of two fundamental ways. Your employer pays you for your work; you buy groceries; you build a fence to keep in the dog; you take a holiday in Tuscany. Transactions of this sort form the bread-and-butter of our daily economic lives, and serve to transfer wealth from one person to another along the links in the network. This is one mechanism by which our wealth goes up or down.

When wealth flows from one person to another, however, the total amount doesn't change. And yet wealth can also be created or destroyed. Say you purchased a house in the UK in 1995. Today, you are probably happy to see that its value has skyrocketed in the recent real-estate boom. Your total wealth has gone up. On the other hand, in 1998, you may have invested some spare cash into the stock market – perhaps even buying shares in Enron or Worldcom – and gone on to read the daily newspapers with a sense of unfolding doom. Investments lead both to the creation and the destruction of wealth.

From this extremely simple perspective, then, two basic factors control the dynamics of wealth. This is hardly contentious, and it may also seem unworthy of consideration. Yet, as physicists Jean-Philippe Bouchaud and Marc Mézard of the University of Paris have recently shown, the interplay of these two basic forces goes a long way to determining how wealth is distributed.[5]

For a network of interacting individuals, Bouchaud and Mézard formulated a set of equations that could follow wealth as it shifts from person to person, and as each person receives random gains or losses from his investments. They also included one further feature to reflect the fact that the value of wealth is relative. A single parent trying to work and raise her son might face near ruin over the loss of a £20 note; in contrast, a very rich person wouldn't flinch after losing a few thousand. In other words, the value of a little more or less wealth depends on how much one already has. This implies that when it comes to investing, wealthy people will tend to invest proportionally more than the less wealthy.

The equations that capture these basic economic processes are quite simple. However, there is a catch. For a network of many people – say, 1,000 or more – the number of equations is similarly large. For this reason, a model of this sort lies well beyond anyone's mathematical abilities to solve (and this explains why it has not appeared in conventional economics). But the philosopher Daniel Dennett has for good reason called digital computers 'the most important epistemological advance in scientific method since the invention of accurate timekeeping devices' and Bouchaud's and Mézard's work falls into a rapidly growing area known as 'computational economics' which exploits the computer to discover principles of economics that one might never identify otherwise.

Bouchaud and Mézard explored their model in an exhaustive series of simulations. And in every run they found the same result – after wealth flows around the network for some time, it falls into a steady pattern in which the basic shape of wealth distribution follows the form discovered by Pareto. Indeed, this happens even when every person starts with exactly the same amount of money and money-making skills. This pattern appears to emerge as a balance between two competing tendencies.

On the one hand, transactions between people tend to spread wealth around. If one person becomes terrifically wealthy, he or she may start businesses, build houses and consume more products, and in each case wealth will tend to flow out to others in the network. Likewise, if one person becomes terrifically poor, less wealth will flow through links going away from him, as he or she will tend to purchase fewer products. Overall, the flow of funds along links in the network should act to wash away wealth disparities.

But it seems that this washing-out effect never manages to gain the upper hand, for the random returns on investment drive a counter-balancing 'rich-get-richer' phenomenon. Even if everyone starts out equally, and all remain equally adept at choosing investments, differences in investment luck will cause some people to accumulate more wealth than others. Those who are lucky will tend to invest more and so have a chance to make greater gains still. Hence, a string of positive returns builds a person's wealth not merely by addition but by multiplication, as each subsequent gain grows ever bigger. This is enough, even in a world of equals where returns on investment are entirely random, to stir up huge wealth disparities in the population.

This finding suggests that the basic inequality in wealth distribution seen in most societies – and globally as well, among nations – may have little to do with differences in the backgrounds and talents of individuals or countries. Rather, the disparity appears as a law of economic life that emerges naturally as an organisational feature of a network. This finding suggests that the temptation to find complex explanations behind the distribution of wealth may be seriously misguided.

Altering inequality

However, this does not imply that there is no possibility for mitigating inequities in wealth. There is some further subtlety to the picture. From an empirical point of view, Pareto found (as many other researchers have found later) that the basic mathematical form of the wealth distribution is the same in all countries. One always finds that each time you double the amount of wealth, the number of people having that much falls by a constant factor. This is the pattern that always leads to a small fraction of the wealthy possessing a large fraction of everything. Nevertheless, the 'constant factor' can be somewhat different from one case to another. The degree of inequity can vary from country to country, and, socially speaking, there's a huge difference between the richest 5 per cent owning 40 per cent of the wealth or their owning 95 per cent.

An additional strength of Bouchaud's and Mézard's network model is that it shows how the degree of inequity in an economy can be altered. They found two general rules. First, the greater the volume of wealth flowing through the economy – the greater the 'vigour' of trading, if you will – then the greater the equality. Conversely, the more volatile the investment returns, the greater the inequity. This has some curious practical implications – some obvious and some not so obvious.

Take taxes, for instance. The model confirms the assumption that income taxes will tend to erode differences in wealth, as long as those taxes are redistributed across the society in a more or less equal way. After all, taxation represents the artificial addition of some extra transactional links into the network, along which wealth can flow from the rich towards the poor. Similarly, a rise in capital gains taxes will also tend to ameliorate wealth disparities, both by discouraging speculation and by decreasing the returns from it. On the other hand, the model suggests that sales taxes, even those targeted at luxury goods, might well exaggerate differences in wealth by leading to fewer sales (thus reducing the number of transactional links) and encouraging people to invest more of their money.

The model also offers an excellent test of some arguments that politicians use to justify policies. In Britain and in the United States, for example, the 1980s and 1990s were dominated by free-market ideology, much of it defended by the idea that wealth would 'trickle down' to the poor. Everything was done to encourage investment activity, regardless of the risks involved. This was the era of junk bonds, the savings and loan debacle, and the dot-com boom, now capped off by the Enron-led wave of corporate scandals. As we know, the wealth did not trickle down and the distribution of wealth in both countries is today significantly less equitable than it was three decades ago. Under the network model, this is just what one would expect – a dramatic increase in investment activity, unmatched by measures to boost the flow of funds between people, ought to kick up an increase in wealth inequality. (Indeed, taxes were also generally lowered during this era, thus removing some of the links that could have helped to redistribute wealth.)

What about globalisation? From the perspective of this model, international trade should offer a means to create a better balance between the richer and poorer nations. Leaving aside legitimate concerns over a lack of environmental regulations, protection for child labourers and so on, Western corporations setting up manufacturing plants in developing nations and exporting their computing and accounting to places like India and the Philippines should help wealth flow into these countries. In some cases, this promise of globalisation has been realised. But, in view of the potential benefits, it is easy to understand the anger of the poorer nations at measures designed to skew the trading network in favour of the richer countries. As Stiglitz comments:

> *The critics of globalization accuse Western countries of hypocrisy, and the critics are right. The Western countries have pushed poor countries to eliminate trade barriers, but kept up their own barriers, preventing developing countries from exporting their agricultural products and so depriving them of desperately needed export income...The West has driven the globalization agenda, ensuring that it garners a disproportionate share of the benefits, at the expense of the developing world.*[6]

As Bouchaud's and Mézard's model illustrates, free trade could be a good thing for everyone, but only if it enables wealth to flow in both directions without bias.

But let's go back to the model, for it also reveals another rather alarming prospect. In further investigations, Bouchaud and Mézard found that if the volatility of investment returns becomes sufficiently great, the wealth differences it churns up can completely overwhelm the natural diffusion of wealth generated by transactions. In such a case, an economy – whether within one nation, or more globally – can undergo a transition wherein its wealth, instead of being held by a small minority, condenses into the pockets of a mere handful of super-rich 'robber barons'.

It is intriguing to wonder if some countries, particularly developing nations, may already be in this state. It has been estimated, for example, that the richest 40 people in Mexico have nearly 30 per cent of the wealth. It could be, also, that many societies went through this phase in the past. Long-term economic trends during the twentieth century lend some credence to this idea, as the total share of the richest individuals in England, for example, has fallen over the last century.

In Russia, following the collapse of the USSR, wealth has become spectacularly concentrated; inequality there is dramatically higher than in any country in the West. The model would suggest that both increased investment volatility and lack of opportunities for wealth redistribution might be at work. In the social vacuum created by the end of the Soviet era, economic activity is less restricted than in the West, as there are few regulations to protect the environment or to provide safety for workers. This not only leads to pollution and human exploitation but also generates extraordinary profits for a few companies (the politically well connected, especially – a popular pun in Russia equates privatisation with the 'grabbing of state assets'). Economists have also pointed out that Russia has been slow to implement income taxes that would help to redistribute wealth.

This simple model is, of course, not the final word in explaining the distribution of wealth or how best to manage it. But it does offer a few basic lessons. Although wealth inequity may indeed be inevitable to a certain extent, its degree can be adjusted. With proper regulation to protect the environment and workers' rights, free trade and globalisation should be forces for good, offering better economic opportunities for all. But we will achieve such happier ends only if global integration is carried out sensibly, carefully and, most of all, honestly. If it is not, and if the disparity between the haves and have-nots continues to grow, then one might expect countervailing social forces to be stirred up, as they have throughout history.

By starting with remarkably simple assumptions and studying the patterns that emerge in a network of interacting agents, Bouchaud and Mézard have gained an important insight into one of the most basic – and contentious – patterns of economic life. Unfortunately, their model by itself cannot help us make wise use of this insight.

Mark Buchanan is a science writer. His most recent book is Small World: uncovering nature's hidden networks. *A version of this essay first appeared in* New Statesman.

Notes

1   J K Galbraith, *A History of Economics* (London: Penguin, 1991).
2   J Flemming and J Micklewright, 'Income distribution, economic systems and transition', Innocenti Occasional Papers, Economic and Social Policy Series, no 70 (Florence: UNICEF International Child Development Centre, 1999).
3   P Krugman, 'An unequal exchange' in *The Accidental Theorist* (New York: Norton, 1998).
4   J Stiglitz, *Globalization and its Discontents* (London: Allen Lane, 2002).
5   J-P Bouchaud and M Mézard, 'Wealth condensation in a simple model of economy', *Physica A*, 282 (2000).
6   Stiglitz, *Globalization and its Discontents*.

Women's networks represent a force for change and social agency with the potential to tackle persistent workplace inequalities . . .

Old boys and new girls

Helen McCarthy

DEM☺S

9. Old boys and new girls

women's networks and diversity in the workplace

Helen McCarthy

Hightech-Women meets on the first Wednesday of every month at the Women's University Club, located in an elegant nineteenth-century brick building in Mayfair. It is an unusual mix of capsule wardrobes, mobile phones, wood-panelled walls and floral-patterned carpets. And yet, the union of these two women's organisations with very different styles could not be more fitting. The club was established in 1883 for the growing numbers of women entering higher education and the professions; today, it also provides a meeting place for a network of ambitious women in technology-related occupations, first brought together by venture capitalist Lucy Marcus in 2000. Hightech-Women's members might be very different from their Victorian and Edwardian forebears, but they exhibit every bit as much appetite for pooling their collective resources in a much changed but still unequal world. Or, for what an early advocate of the women's networking movement simply describes as 'getting together to get ahead'.[1]

Hightech-Women is one of a growing movement of networks creating professional communities of women across many sectors. Yet this phenomenon is little understood and sparsely documented. This essay, based on emerging findings from a Demos research project, sets out to understand how women's networks function and to explore the contribution they might make to equality and diversity goals in a so-called 'post-feminist' era.

A brief history of women's networks

Women in Britain have associated in various ways for many centuries, often forming strong personal ties through the relationships that characterise women's traditional, domestically oriented roles. These sorts of relationships between women still exist today to varying degrees. However, what is analytically distinctive about the peer-to-peer networking activities described in this essay is the way in which they give a formal expression and visibility to previously informal and loosely organised relationships, and focus them around a gendered professional identity. Women's networks thus can complicate professional identities by constructing alternative narratives of and generating new perspectives about organisations. In doing so, they represent a force for organisational change and a form of social agency with the potential to tackle persistent workplace inequalities between women and men.

Communities of professional women began to grow at the end of the nineteenth century when various membership associations and institutions were founded for the rising number of women entering Britain's universities and professions. However, it was not until the 1970s, the period in which sexual politics were put firmly back on the political agenda by the Women's Liberation Movement, that the dynamic peer-to-peer networking model recognisable among professional women today began to take shape. Small groups of businesswomen began to meet together in cities in the UK and the US, initially through low-key gatherings for breakfast or lunch. These grew rapidly into large corporate networks based within companies, or external business networks with a nationwide reach.[2]

These early networks set the trend for those that followed. The activities ranged from purely social gatherings to workshops, seminars, mentoring programmes and opportunities for voluntary work, supplemented with access to general advice, information and mutual support through the network. This model was adopted in the UK by women in professions beyond the business world steadily throughout the 1980s. However, over the last five to ten years, Britain has witnessed what might be understood as a 'new wave' of the women's networking movement. This coincided with – indeed constituted part of – a new self-confidence experienced by women, especially among young professional women, in the 1990s. This decade witnessed growing evidence of a generational shift in attitudes towards more flexible and fluid gender roles, as well as the disruption of traditional feminist narratives of women's collective consciousness and political mobilisation.[3] The 'new girl networks', as they were light-heartedly described, reflected elements of this new gender politics. Networks bubbled up in sectors as diverse as technology (DigitalEve), journalism (Women in Journalism), small business (Women into the Network) and corporate social responsibility (CSR Chicks). Many of these have youthful memberships, are highly proactive in marketing themselves externally with sophisticated brand identities, funky websites and catchy names, and make effective use of the internet as a communications and community-building tool.

Over the same period, large employers have begun to explore networks as an alternative to conventional equal opportunities and centrally owned diversity initiatives, the limitations of which are becoming more widely understood. 'Corporate networks' provide opportunities for women in organisations to lead their own professional development and contribute to the strengthening of gender diversity in the workplace. Lloyds TSB, GE, Citigroup and Shell have all launched corporate women's networks in the last five years, and diversity networks are a growing presence too within the civil service and the wider public sector. These internal networks not only connect women within the organisation, but provide important advice and intelligence to the management on women's needs, and in many cases help to design and implement diversity policies.

Selection of UK women's networks

Women in Management 1969
City Women's Network 1978
Women in Business and Finance 1980

Women in Medicine 1980
Network 1981
Women in BP 1982
Women in Dentistry 1985
BT Women's Network 1986
Women Chemists Network 1988
Through the Glass Ceiling 1990
Women in Journalism 1995
Berwin Leighton Paisner/The Adelaide Group 1997
Everywoman 1999
CSR Chicks 1999
Lloyds TSB Women's Network 1999
Busygirl 2000 (renamed Aurora Women's Network in 2003)
Hightech-Women 2000
DigitalEve 2000
Financial Mail Women's Forum 2001
Citiwomen (Citigroup) 2002
Thinkingwomen 2002
Senior Civil Service Women's Network 2001
Shell Women's Network UK 2003
BT Senior Women's Network 2003
Dynamic Asian Women's Network (DAWN) 2003

New opportunities and old inequalities

So what accounts for this current flurry of interest around networks? It is undoubtedly in part a reflection of the greater clout that women wield in their working lives. The rising numbers of corporate networks suggests growing recognition among employers of the case for developing women's talent as a core business strategy. This perspective is particularly well advanced in the US, where research shows how corporate women's networks have helped large companies to decrease turnover and increase productivity as well as enhance equality and diversity in their organisations.[4]

Nevertheless, women's networks are also a symptom of another, less celebratory aspect of women's working lives. Alongside the unprecedented opportunities now available to them, women continue to experience gender-related disadvantage in their status in the workforce. For example, women working full-time earn on average 18.8 per cent less than the average hourly earnings of male full-time employees. They make up just 9 per cent of directors in FTSE 100 companies, 13 per cent of small business owners and 23 per cent of top managers in the civil service,[5] yet account for 79 per cent of administrative and secretarial occupations.[6] At the same time women continue to work a 'second shift' by taking on the lion's share of domestic work and childcare.[7]

In their *modus operandi* women's networks hold a mirror up to this phenomenon of growing opportunity and persisting inequality. While celebrating women's achievements and advancements, many, either explicitly or implicitly, hold women's continuing under-representation and lack of progression in their chosen field as major points of reference. Underlying this position is the normative assumption that women are disadvantaged relative to men in building successful careers, and this basic narrative of inequality is what thus justifies the existence of women-centred initiatives, such as networks. To this extent, women's networks might be accurately described as 'feminist' organisations, although few would choose to describe their activities in these terms. Indeed, this distancing from the ideological legacy of second-wave feminism may well be one of the greatest strengths of women's networks, in that they provide a model of affiliation and mutual support which has wide appeal, especially to younger women.

Old boys and new girls

A concern with the position of women in the labour market is not unique to women's networks, and is shared with any number of policy-makers, academics and pressure groups working in this field. It remains to be asked then: what is special or distinctive about peer-to-peer networks as an organisational form for achieving change in this area? Or, to put it another way, why do networks matter when it comes to inequality?

The answer lies in the role of networks in distributing power, resources and opportunity across a wider system. Historically, patterns of social connectivity have been instrumental in the production and reproduction of gender disadvantage, an idea most commonly expressed in the phrase the 'old boy network' (OBN). When first coined in the mid-nineteenth century, this phrase referred specifically to the alumni of an elite educational institution, whose shared educational backgrounds and common affiliations naturally translated into an informal system of favours and mutual support throughout later life.

Although these types of networks still exist and retain some influence in certain quarters, as a concept, the OBN has gained a wider meaning as familiar shorthand for *all* forms of male power in public life and the workplace. Today, the patterns of social connectivity among men that are of most concern for equality in Britain's workplaces are less likely to be tied to the public school or the gentleman's club than ever before. Instead, they tend to reflect embedded forms of sociability that do not formally exclude women but, combined with unequal caring roles in the home and women's often asymmetrical working patterns, contribute to the concentration of power in male hands. In other words, these processes often create organisational cultures that value and reward qualities or behaviours that women are less likely to exhibit than men; that require, as US law professor Susan Estrich puts it, women's 'adaptation to a male comfort zone'.[8]

In this sense, the new girl networks are not mirror images of their male counterparts, as is sometimes supposed. While many supporters believe that women can and should employ some of the same tactics as the OBN, particularly with regard to using one's contacts instrumentally, few networks aspire to achieving the same hegemony for women that men have traditionally enjoyed in the workplace. Women's networks have transparent structures and formal status, and exist primarily for the purpose of supporting women's networking practices. In contrast, the institutions that nurture social ties among men do not tend to hold networking as their formal or explicit aim.

Furthermore, women's networks should be understood as being fundamentally concerned with altering social relations, rather than preserving them. Just as it is useful to view patterns of social connectivity among men through the filter of power relations, it is also helpful to see women's networks as a disruptive force impacting upon those relations. By actively creating opportunities for women to extend their personal and professional networks, women's networks alter the dynamics of the patterns of social ties established by men, and create alternative spaces in which male norms and behaviours can be challenged. Directed in the right way, women's networks thus have the potential to create more inclusive working environments for all. For example, the GE Women's Network allows men to attend meetings as a way of drawing them into conversation about the dynamics of gender in the workplace and how managers can treat employees of both sexes fairly. In its early years of existence, the Lloyds TSB Women's Network developed a set of professional development tools for its members, which were eventually adopted by Human Resources and taken into the mainstream of the core programme offered to all employees.

The missing link in equality strategies?

These insights have much to offer the current debate on the future of gender equality. For much of the last 30 years, the legislative and policy instruments of the state have been regarded as the most effective way to protect individuals from discrimination and to compensate for historical disparities of power. Over the past decade this framework has been challenged by the 'business case for equality' – an approach that attempts to link equality goals with workplace diversity and business objectives. Thus business imperatives, in theory at least, remove the need for coercion or heavy regulation by the state. While the 'business case' approach is widely recognised by policy-makers and employers, concerned voices from the equality lobby point to slow rates of progress and the failure of 'soft' tools to embed equality and diversity perspectives throughout organisational cultures and working practices. As a result, today the debate often becomes trapped within an unhelpful dichotomy of compulsion versus voluntarism.

The major problem with this dichotomy is that it cannot accommodate any approach to equality that doesn't take either the state or the market as its starting point. Yet policy-makers are increasingly recognising that long-term problems cannot be addressed using the traditional instruments available to them, or by a blind faith in market forces. Instead, as Bentley and Wilsdon have recently argued, they require changing the dominant assumptions governing models of organisation, and the development of greater adaptive capacity at every level of the system.[9] In this emerging framework, gender inequality should be understood as a problem involving complex, dynamic processes that cannot be easily tackled by reference to existing models or off-the-peg solutions. Instead, it requires open-ended capacity-building efforts, involving multiple stakeholders, across the wider system, which produces and reproduces gender inequalities. Women's networks might not provide the whole picture here, but they offer some important clues as to what an 'adaptive' approach towards gender equality could look like.

An approach that is participatory

Equality cannot be 'gifted' to individuals or groups by the state using a top-down model, nor can it be bestowed by diversity initiatives driven by employers. These approaches are least likely to win widespread legitimacy and most likely to attract backlash and charges of tokenism. In contrast, the starting point for women's networks is women themselves. Whether corporate or sector-wide, networks rely on the active participation of their members to succeed. They facilitate access to a supportive and enabling community, but individuals have the ultimate responsibility for converting the ties they make through the network into concrete opportunities and outcomes. Women's success is thus generated by women's own agency.

An approach that is self-organising

In the same way that equality and diversity initiatives that are imposed in a top-down manner are unlikely to result in whole system change, women's networks cannot be prescribed by managers. The first corporate networks were created on the initiative of individual women who perceived a need, and succeeded because there was a groundswell of women within the company who shared that view. The same principle applies to networks outside the workplace, where the range and scope of activities tend to be member-led, often evolving through series of experiments and listening exercises. This self-organising quality gives networks their dynamic quality, but it may also explain why some networks do not survive.

An approach that accommodates diversity

The fragmentation of the women's movement during the 1980s is often attributed to the challenge of diversity. Women's identities and experiences, it was felt by many, were far too complex and diverse to sustain any notion of collective interests, and the search for consensus thus became an illegitimate political project. Today, women's networks offer an alternative model of solidarity, which balances the interests of individuals ('What can I get out of this? How can I develop as a person?') with the desire for reciprocity, mutual support and, if appropriate, collective action ('How can I help others? What can we achieve together?'). Women's networks are highly flexible, allowing members to pick and choose how and when they connect with each other. Many women are members of several networks simultaneously, or switch from one to another as their needs change. While networks create shared identities among women, they do not demand political consensus.

An approach that operates on several levels simultaneously

Gender inequality cannot be tackled by breaking the problem down into smaller components and treating each one separately. Rather, a fabric of interrelated factors must be addressed at the same time. Women's networks operate on at least three levels. First, they meet the needs of individuals for professional development and community. Second, by developing women's talent, they contribute to diversity within workplaces and promote the progression of women across sectors and, through this, women's networks have the potential to strengthen the overall performance of an organisation or sector.

Emerging questions

This initial exploration of women's networks points to a cluster of questions that warrant further consideration. The first centres on the processes of change within organisations, and the sort of contribution that diversity networks, with their dynamic, peer-to-peer structures, can make to learning and managing knowledge, capacity-building and developing trust within communities of practice. The second focuses on the interface between women's networks and other social institutions. Viewed through the lens of their campaigning and voluntary work and, in many cases, their strong grassroots presence in local communities, to what extent are women's networks agents of 'social capital' and civic participation? And what do they tell us about the role of gender in community-building processes? The final set of questions concerns the nature of the policy challenge: how can we identify a role for policy-makers in supporting and nurturing women's networks as part of a wider, 'adaptive' approach to gender equality? As such, this essay represents an overture to a much richer, ongoing conversation about the contribution of diversity networks in creating inclusive workplaces for all.

Helen McCarthy is a researcher at Demos, and is co-founder of women's network thinkingwomen. *She is also author of the forthcoming Demos publication* Girlfriends in High Places, *which will be published in April 2004.*

Notes

1   M Scott Welch, *Networking: the great new way for women to get ahead* (New York: Harcourt Brace Jovanovich, 1980).

2   For an overview of these developments, see Scott Welch, *Networking*.
3   H Wilkinson, M Howard and S Gregory, *Tomorrow's Women* (London: Demos, 1997); H Wilkinson, *No Turning Back: generations and the genderquake* (London: Demos, 1995).
4   Catalyst Women in Business, *Creating Women's Networks: a how-to guide for women and companies* (San Francisco, CA: Jossey-Bass, 1998).
5   Equal Opportunities Commission, *Sex and Power: who runs Britain?* (Manchester: EOC, 2004).
6   Equal Opportunities Commission, *Facts about Women and Men in Great Britain* (Manchester: EOC, 2003).
7   A Jones, *About Time for Change* (London: Work Foundation, 2003).
8   S Estrich, *Sex and Power* (New York: Riverhead Books, 2000).
9   T Bentley and J Wilsdon, 'Introduction' in *The Adaptive State* (London: Demos, 2003).

Almost every aspect of life that citizens care about is affected by the patterns, nature and distribution of social ties between people . . .

Your friendship networks

Dr Perri 6

DEMOS

10. Your friendship networks

are they any of the government's business?

Dr Perri 6

Networks of friendship and acquaintance among citizens matter to government.[1] Almost every aspect of life that citizens care about and want government to tackle is affected by the patterns, the nature and the distribution of social ties between people. Your chances of catching the common cold as well as many other aspects of health status are significantly affected by the extent of your social support. Getting out of unemployment is most often achieved using informal ties to find work. The pathways into crime are best traced along the connections young people have to those already involved in criminal activities. Educational attainment is hugely affected by the culture of attainment among your peers. We get through the grief of bereavement better for being supported. Remaining independent into old age rests greatly on being able to draw upon friends and neighbours and not just on close relatives.

So it is hardly surprising that policy-makers are interested. But can government do anything deliberately to influence our patterns of friendship and acquaintance? And indeed, should it, or is a step too far towards the intrusive, authoritarian state? Should friendship and acquaintance be off-limits to policy-makers?

Government shapes whom we meet

Certainly, almost everything that government does has an unavoidable impact on our personal social networks. Housing design, slum clearance and transport policy bring some people together and keep others apart, and make it easier or harder for them to reach each other. The now 50-year-long debate about tower blocks and 'communities' is really a debate about the ways in which government shapes patterns of friendship and acquaintance. Education famously creates ties between pupils and students that can sometimes last for a lifetime. Whether social services are provided in ways that bring people with similar problems together (think of special day centres for people with mental health problems, or lunch clubs for older people) or whether they are organised around providing services to people individually, these decisions greatly affect the chances of forming and sustaining certain types of bonds. When government offers job clubs and special training programmes to unemployed people to help them seek work, they tend to meet mainly other unemployed people, who may be the least useful to them in seeking work by informal means. Nonetheless, these services can significantly affect whom users get the chance to meet.

So it is hard to see how government could do other than have a huge effect on our social networks. Even the 'minimal' or 'night-watchman' state advocated by neoliberals would have a huge impact, both in the process of dismantling the apparatus of civil government, and in the ways in which people would have to adapt. As Polanyi argued 60 years ago, free markets are only ever created by government action, which itself brings about massive change to social networks.[2]

Networks as an objective of policy?

Public services inevitably and vastly influence our networks in unintended ways. But may government legitimately, and can it feasibly, deliberately and directly pursue specific policy goals to influence friendship and acquaintance? Or, in other words, does government do better or worse, and does it violate fewer rights or more, when it tries consciously and with care to achieve something that it will affect massively in any case?

These are questions that ought to be addressed seriously before governments rush to develop 'social capital building' programmes. One key problem is that all the good things in social life do not go together, and different types of networks generate different sorts of outcomes, which must be better understood. For example, the kinds of social networks that conduce to thriving in the labour market tend to be quite open, stressing acquaintance with people in situations different from one's own. By contrast, the networks that help people in later life tend to be more bounded, dense networks where all those who provide support know each other and share linked lives. In another context, the network forms which characterise neighbourhood renewal efforts are often marked by dense ties among the residents of a tightly defined neighbourhood. These may well not be conducive to the kinds of local economic development processes that are most important for improving an area's connections with the surrounding travel-to-work area. If governments are to try to influence their citizens' friendships and acquaintances deliberately, they must first of all acknowledge the need for trade-offs between different types of networks. Then policy-makers have the choice of focusing on the special cases where only one type of network is beneficial, or else on trying to balance different forms.

Network types

It is helpful to offer a framework for classifying the basic types of social networks, so that we can at least identify the elements between which trade-offs might have to be struck. It has been argued that there are four basic types of networks (see Figure 1):[3]

Individualistic networks, which are sparse but open, allow for the kinds of entrepreneurial and instrumental use of ties that link one to people very different from oneself. This, then, is the freewheeling world of the promotion-hungry 'networker'. *Enclaved networks*, by contrast, are dense but strongly bounded and tend to reinforce ties to those similarly situated. Here is where we find the mutual support clubs and some inward-looking 'communities'.

Hierarchical networks are also bounded, but link people with very different powers and resources in more rule-bound ways. This describes the kinds of ties that link people to those formally allocated to mentor or counsel them, or the informal ties that link many chairs of tenants' associations with the town hall professionals who make decisions about investments in their housing estates.

Isolate networks, the final type, are not necessarily those in which people know literally no other people, but rather the mix of sparse and casual ties to others with a few very close ties perhaps to immediate family members, but which admit of very little reliable support beyond immediate needs and afford little scope for collective action.

Each of these network types has its strengths and its weaknesses. Individualism is useful in many labour market situations; hierarchical networks are valuable in some educational settings; and enclaves can be very supportive for people who find themselves rejected by mainstream institutions. Even the isolate form has its uses, for it provides a way of coping during adversity.

Do governments know how to make a difference?

Assuming (a very big if) that governments can know better than citizens themselves what network forms ought to be promoted, what tools could they deploy through public services to cultivate among citizens some beneficial mix of these types? And how could these tools be deployed without violating rights such as liberty and privacy?

Past measures used in various public services to influence social networks have a mixed record of success. Comprehensive schooling and mixed tenure schemes are examples of interventions that have not been terribly effective in promoting the kinds of social network structures that policy-makers have hoped from them,[4] although it is possible that they might be more efficacious when used in social contexts which are initially more communitarian in their institutions. The evidence (to the extent that we have been able to interpret it) is equivocal regarding the efficacy of excluding pupils from schools, funding voluntary organisations and setting up 'buddying' schemes in influencing social networks in Western countries. This may be either because the effects may be modest, because the effects do not last, or

Figure 1 Network signatures of the basic institutional forms of social organisation

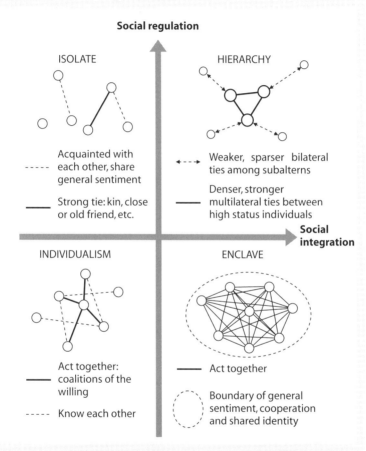

The network forms in the top half of this diagram exhibit more bilateral ties, with those in the bottom half exhibiting more multilateral ties. Similarly, those to the left involve a lower ongoing mutual dependence for material resources and support, with those to the right involving a higher mutual dependence.

because the intervention may provoke significant counter-organisation towards other network forms. The impact of other types of government action, such as life skills training and job clubs, we simply do not know. Figure 2 shows the distribution of a range of initiatives identified by the kind of solidarity that they might have promoted if they were effective, and what we currently know about their actual effectiveness.[5]

The evidence available in the literature[6] suggests that, so far at least, public services have yet to develop very sophisticated tools on which to build any grand strategy for deliberate network shaping. The evaluative literature is very thin indeed. It hardly considers the interaction effects of the combinations of multiple measures as they affect the same groups of people and is weak in examining unintended consequences. In addition, it does not really examine the extent to which privacy concerns are being respected or the extent to which professionals are using these tools to gain greater discretionary power. Some evaluative instruments have been developed, especially in the field of care for frail older people (by Clare Wenger and her collaborators[7]), that attempt to capture the impact of services upon client's social networks, but they are still not being widely used.

Very often people advocate fashionable measures for which the evidence of sustained impact on the social networks of their clients is largely missing. Robert Putnam has famously argued for much more generous public subsidy for voluntary organisations in the belief that they will conduce to 'social capital' – by which he means almost any kind of network other than the isolate form; he does not seem to accept that there are incompatibilities between these network forms that require trade-offs and even tough choices between them.[8] However, there is really very little evidence that the social networks of clients of voluntary bodies are influenced in any lasting way by using their services, and the few studies that have been conducted actually suggest that, if there are effects, they are short-lived.[9] Even religious bodies, said by some to be better at stimulating ties, actually turn out in the few studies done to be no more impressive than comparable government services.[10]

Figure 2 Interventions by solidarities they are designed to promote

Social regulation

ISOLATE

† Segregation of individual offenders within institutions
? † School exclusion without readmission to another school

HIERARCHY

? Counselling
? Life skills training
Mentoring
† Funding voluntary organisations
? Circles of support
† Designing out crime, e.g. closing streets to block criminals' escape routes
? † City centre pedestrianisation; zoning for street cafés and clubs
School exclusion into speciality units

Social integration

INDIVIDUALISM

? Life skills training
Entrepreneurs' networks
Business borrowers' clubs
* Comprehensive schooling
* Mixed tenure schemes

ENCLAVE

Segregated allocation of social rented housing
† Buddying schemes
Befriending schemes
† Funding voluntary organisations
Drop-in centres
? Job clubs
Communal spaces for residents in defined small areas
? † City centre pedestrianisation; zoning for street cafés and clubs
* ? Creating local non-profit organisations

* Interventions which the evidence suggests have not been effective in promoting the kinds of social network structures that policy-makers had hoped from them.
† Interventions where the evidence about their efficacy in changing social networks is equivocal. Effects may not last, may be modest, or the intervention may provoke counter-organisation towards other solidarities.
? Interventions that may or may not in practice conduce to that solidarity.

Certainly, if we are interested in the promotion of ties between the worse off and the better off – which is important in stimulating labour market mobility – then there is no evidence that voluntary bodies are any more effective in this than are comparable public bodies. Furthermore, social services agencies are less effective than education bodies, irrespective of sector. While membership of voluntary bodies may be associated with attitudes such as willingness to trust others,[11] it is far from clear that membership causes any change in attitudes: associations may well typically recruit people who are already readier to trust others.

Interestingly, the evaluative studies do suggest that the most effective interventions are the least direct and the least coercive. For example, support for voluntary social networks of local small business entrepreneurs has been found effective in stimulating the kinds of typically individualistic networks that can help in local economic development. In addition, providing life skills training to those least able to form friendships and acquaintances for various reasons appears often to be capable of making a significant difference at the individual level. Least effective in influencing social networks in any lasting way appear to be the many interventions whereby public services provide an 'artificial friend' such as a mentor, or a specially created group (these measures may have other merits, of course). Physical measures to change architecture and town layout tend to be effective mainly in the negative sense that certain kinds of crime can be made more difficult, and certain spaces more easily surveyed by residents. However, their effects on actual social networks seem not to be very great, and least significant in respect of forming new ties that would not otherwise have been created.

The policy challenge

Moreover, implementing such measures can be very challenging. The skills required are not always available. Indeed, some public service professions have been reformed in recent years precisely to shift their work away from influencing patterns of social networks. Social work has increasingly focused on practical support for older people and protective interventions for children. Probation has been directed towards more supervisory work, such as risk assessment, cognitive behavioural interventions at the individual level and enforcement, and away from its traditional role in shaping the social aspects of rehabilitation. The pastoral role of teaching has been squeezed by the need to focus on curriculum delivery and maintaining discipline. While new skills for helping people to cultivate networks may be emerging in neighbourhood renewal work, and perhaps even among some employment advisers, they are hardly formalised, trained or valued as such.

It is also clear that the tools for shaping social networks are better developed in those services that work with the least advantaged. For those who think that public services should always be targeted upon the worst off, and for those who think that problems about social networks mainly affect the poorest, perhaps this is not a problem. But government should be concerned about the extent to which the least well-off can use their networks to access people who are better off than themselves, not only for instrumental reasons to do with seeking work, but also to avoid the deepening mutual enclaving of the social classes in respect of social ties that tends to follow whenever any society goes through a period of growing income and wealth inequality combined with high levels of fear of crime. In this context, the limited nature of the toolkit with which government can address the social ties of the better-off might well be a matter of some concern.[12]

This suggests that government ought to be very cautious before advocating ambitious policies for 'promoting social capital', as some enthusiastic researchers and even some policy advocates in the World Bank have been doing.[13] This is not only out of suspicion of grand social engineering projects in general but, more practically, because policy-makers ought to recognise how little we really know about how public services can develop sets of practices that might have lasting influence on the social networks of service users and non-users alike. In addition, they must recognise how far we are from understanding how to strike trade-offs or make intelligent choices between the different types of social networks that government might consider trying to promote.

Conclusion

In this situation it is much more sensible for governments to focus on more modest goals. Specifically, they should surely make it a priority to try to limit the clear harms their interventions do to people's social networks. For example, training programmes for the unemployed that facilitate the creation of ties with other unemployed people only do little to extend those individuals' access to informal routes into work, and may do some harm by way of peer effects on aspirations. Again, it should be clear from recent inquiries that 'care in the community' quickly becomes neglect in the community and 'domiciliary care' can readily become a humane form of house arrest if little or no attention is paid to the social networks of those who use these services. Community development programmes that focus all effort on building ties within a community and fail to address the importance of links outside can quickly reinforce enclaving. It makes far more sense at this stage in our knowledge for governments to be trying to develop piecemeal strategies with which to tackle these network harms. Along with this must go the most careful attention to respecting the privacy of much of the highly sensitive personal information that public bodies and their staff collect about the friendships and acquaintance of their clients. For without reassurance on these matters, the public will rightly be reluctant to trust in governments that seek to influence their social networks.

So, do governments do better by trying to influence the networks of citizens deliberately? Or do they actually do better when they simply provide material services and leave the network consequences where they lie? At the moment, the only answer seems to be that if policy-makers are to do better by trying to coordinate policies and measures deliberately, then they had better begin by being very modest in ambition; by prioritising to limit network harms that flows from public service provision; by recognising that all the good things do not go together; and by accepting that they must care about all – not just one or two – types of networks.

Dr Perri 6 is a senior research fellow at the Health Services Management Centre, University of Birmingham.

Notes

1   This article is based on work for a forthcoming book, Perri 6, *The Politics of Social Cohesion*; see also Perri 6, 'Can government influence our friendships? The range and limits of tools for trying to shape solidarities', in C Phillipson, G Allen and D Morgan (eds), *Social Networks and Social Exclusion: sociological and policy issues* (Aldershot and London: Ashgate, 2003); Perri 6, 'Governing friends and acquaintances: public policy and social networks', in V Nash (ed.), *Reclaiming Community* (London: Institute for Public Policy Research, 2002).

2   K Polanyi, *The Great Transformation: the political and economic origins of our time* (Boston, Mass: Beacon Press, 1944).

3   Perri 6, 'Can government influence our friendships? The range and limits of tools for trying to shape solidarities', in C Phillipson, G Allen and D Morgan (eds), *Social Networks and Social Exclusion: sociological and policy issues* (Aldershot and London: Ashgate, 2003). The taxonomy is based on that of M Douglas, 'Cultural bias', in M Douglas, *In the Active Voice* (London: Routledge and Kegan, 1982) and ultimately on É Durkheim, *Suicide: a study in sociology*, tr. J Spaulding and G Simpson (London: Routledge, 1951 [1897]).

4   This is based on a review of the available literature, but it should be noted that rather little of the research has been principally concerned with evaluating impacts on social networks, and there are many limitations and weaknesses in the studies.

5   Figure 2 refers to the Western world, with its relative aggregate weighting towards greater individualism rather than either of the strongly integrated solidarities. Interventions that seem ineffective in this context might be more efficacious when used in social contexts which are initially more communitarian in their institutions.

6   The full review of the literature will appear in Perri 6, *The Politics of Social Cohesion*, forthcoming.

7   GC Wenger, 'Social networks and the prediction of elderly people at risk', *Aging and Mental Health* 1, no 4 (1997).

8   RE Putnam, *Bowling Alone: the collapse and revival of American community* (New York: Simon and Schuster, 2000).

9   D Stolle, '"Getting to trust": an analysis of the importance of institutions, families, personal experiences and group membership', in P Dekker and EM Uslaner (eds), *Social Capital and Participation in Everyday Life* (London: Routledge, 2001).

10   M Chaves and W Tsitos, 'Congregations and social services: what they do, how

they do it, and with whom', *Nonprofit and Voluntary Sector Quarterly* 30, 4 (2001).

11   M Hooghe and D Stolle (eds) *Generating Social Capital: civil society and institutions in comparative perspective* (Basingstoke: Palgrave, 2003).

12   Perri 6, 'Profiles, networks, risk and hoarding: public policy and the dynamics of social mobility and social cohesion', paper for the Performance and Innovation Unit seminar on social mobility, 20 March 2001.

13   Available at www.worldbank.org/poverty/scapital/; see also S Aldridge, D Halpern and S Fitzpatrick, 'Social capital: a discussion paper', Strategy Unit, Cabinet Office, 2002, available at www.number-10.gov.uk/su/social%20capital/socialcapital.pdf.

If the rhetoric of community-led regeneration is to be translated into real change, then informal networks are crucial to the journey . . .

Developing the well-connected community

Alison Gilchrist

DEM✷S

11. Developing the well-connected community

Alison Gilchrist

Over the recent past, society has become both more informal and more complex. We prefer to live without status and hierarchy, abandoning bureaucratic rules and conventions in favour of more fluid notions of identity, and becoming more flexible about how, and by whom, decisions are made.

These trends are recognised in many current debates about 'community'. Nonetheless, government policies to promote stronger communities and active citizenship have tended to emphasise the role of individuals within formal structures, and, until recently, have overlooked the significance of informal activities within community settings. The related concepts of 'community' and 'networks' must be better understood by policy-makers if they are to avoid the risk of masking common experiences of inequality and discrimination, based on enduring power imbalances and social exclusion.

Government's love affair with 'community'

Strategies for public participation in decision-making date back several decades. The Labour government has simply accelerated this trend with its current emphasis on subsidiarity and partnership working based on community involvement and leadership.[1] Policy debates have often been premised on an image of community as a homogenous and harmonious dimension of social life, securely located within geographical boundaries and anchored by shared values and assumptions. Policy-makers have regarded the idea of community as a panacea for society's ills – a haven where people can find, and express, solidarity and compassion. The term 'community' is used in policy debates to soften the edges of unpalatable programmes and to harness the unpaid energy, expertise and enthusiasm of local volunteers and activists.

The government's interest in 'community' can be broken down in relation to three different but not mutually exclusive goals.

Improving governance

Broad swathes of government policy require public and private agencies to work in partnership arrangements, and to engage with communities in developing and delivering programmes that meet needs and aspirations. Decision-making procedures, led by elected politicians and implemented by public servants, are augmented or displaced by consultative forums and mechanisms for encouraging greater participation and influence among groups who have hitherto been marginalised or alienated by formal political systems. New forms of governance are being devised to support more effective community representation in a concerted attempt to modernise democracy and renovate civil society.

Yet there is still a long way to go in learning how these complex multi-agency structures can manage the interface between communities, programme managers and policy-makers. One key challenge is to understand better the impact of informal networks on what should be transparent and democratic processes.[2] Community representatives report that they feel disempowered by the culture of many partnerships, finding themselves 'out of the loop' of much of the decision-making. While often being excluded from the informal networks where crucial discussions take place, their attendance at partnership meetings also means that they have less time to attend to their own community networks, which provide support and ensure accountability. The resulting frustrations and suspicions can lead to derailment and delays because of the lack of trust among partners and a consequent unwillingness to delegate to delivery agents on the part of policy-makers.

Strengthening social capital

Over the past few years, there has been a burgeoning interest in the concept of 'social capital', a term coined by social scientists to highlight the collective value of the networks of personal relationships and organisational connections. There is a growing body of empirical evidence suggesting that robust and diverse social networks enhance the health and happiness of individuals, and contribute to the well-being of society as a whole. In his well-known book, *Bowling Alone*, Robert Putnam sets out a range of studies linking measures of social capital to educational attainment, economic regeneration, crime reduction and employability.[3] All of these are key themes in the government's neighbourhood renewal agenda and, as a consequence, policy-makers have enthusiastically embraced social capital theory as a possible framework for increasing social inclusion and community cohesion – hence current programmes supporting volunteering, active citizenship and the work of social entrepreneurs. The government is particularly interested in 'bridging' and 'linking' social capital, and recognises the important role that voluntary and community organisations play in this respect.

However, sceptics have raised issues around the social capital approach to strengthening communities, pointing to inequalities operating within networks and arguing that 'norms' can be oppressive for some, while empowering for others. Putnam's studies relied on survey data on civic engagement and membership of voluntary organisations. It has proved much harder, however, to capture the 'connectivity' that this is supposed to reflect, mainly because it has been difficult to collect and analyse evidence on the nature and extent of informal community networks, let alone make an assessment of how these might have changed over time. This is beginning to be addressed through the use of participatory appraisal techniques, where communities undertake their own research into local social capital.[4]

Enhancing service delivery

Communities have always provided a range of services to their own members, through self-help groups and mutual aid. Interpersonal networks, based on trust and need, enable people to access services and resources without an exchange of money or formal contract. These arrangements work when people can be confident that such exchanges are likely to be reciprocated, either directly through returned favours or indirectly through a shared commitment to the 'common good'. Local exchange trading schemes (LETS) and TimeBank initiatives have sought to replicate this networking through the explicit use of tokens or time credits.

Voluntary organisations regard communities as their natural constituency, claiming that they are innovative and sensitive to the requirements of disadvantaged sections of the population that have been neglected by mainstream services. In seeking to tackle social exclusion, the government has looked to strengthen the capacity of the voluntary and community sector to deliver a wider range of services, acknowledging its particular strengths in reaching the hardest to reach. However, even though compacts have been developed to validate and protect the autonomy of voluntary and community organisations, greater partnership working still runs the risk of eroding the independent and pioneering nature of many voluntary organisations. Recent reviews have recommended a targeted increase in resources to the sector, but at the same time called for a rationalisation of intermediary and support bodies in favour of 'front-line' service providers. These trends in funding arrangements may make it less easy for the sector to maintain its flexible, boundary-spanning networks because of the pressure to deliver services and provide formal consultation mechanisms.

These new policy directions acknowledge that communities can contribute to democratic decision-making by adding value to the design, development and delivery of services, and in so doing promote social inclusion and cohesion. However, the rhetoric of participation and partnership has proved difficult to turn into a reality. There has been an over-reliance on voluntary sector

professionals or self-appointed community leaders acting as representatives for the sector, and a failure to allow enough time for
relationships of trust, respect and understanding to develop between
partners and communities. Partnership boards have been under
pressure to spend budgets and find solutions to hitherto intractable
social problems. Unrealistic timescales set by electoral cycles and a
tradition of short-termism have created additional pressures. It is not
surprising that many are experiencing major difficulties in achieving
the ambitious targets set by government.

Developing 'community' networks

Despite this focus on service delivery there has been a growing
realisation that community engagement is not the same as voluntary
sector liaison. Community leaders have often been unpaid and under-
valued activists who are constantly asked to convey the (sometimes
unknown) views of their communities and to defend decisions over
which they feel no sense of ownership. Effective community
involvement in cross-sectoral partnerships can only be sustained,
therefore, on the basis of sufficient organisational capacity and strong
interpersonal connections. Communities are themselves complex and
dynamic, comprising overlapping but shifting networks and alliances,
used by communities to promote or defend their interests in an ever-
changing environment. Communities exist where there is interaction
and mutual influence. Social networks express and reinforce a sense
of belonging, of mutuality, based on somewhat transient notions of
'us' and 'them'. To varying extents, community networks comprise
neighbours, work colleagues, fellow activists, those who might share a
faith or hobby, or people who have faced similar experiences, for
example, through migration or discrimination. If this is the case, then
how can networks be shaped to contribute to stronger, more inclusive
communities?

The well-connected community

In the first instance, it is important to acknowledge that communities
have always contained differences and divisions, even where these

have been hidden under a veneer of conformity or 'respectability'. Tensions are an inescapable part of community life, and the capacity to resolve conflicts is essential for a cohesive and inclusive society. As Fritjof Capra recognises in his model of the 'web of life', ethnic and cultural diversity plays the same role in human societies as that of ecological diversity in ecosystems. A diverse community is resilient, with the capacity to adapt to changing situations: 'However, diversity is a strategic advantage only if there is a truly vibrant community, sustained by a web of relationships. If the community is fragmented into isolated groups and individuals, diversity can easily become a source of prejudice and friction.'[5]

We actively and symbolically construct communities according to the conditions we find, the challenges that we encounter and the choices we make. Many communities organise themselves along lines that perpetuate injustice and segregation. Traditions and structures are overly rigid and social connections simply repeat patterns of informal interaction among people who are broadly similar or who obey conventional mores. Such communities are often isolated and unwilling to adapt to change. They become stagnant, defending themselves against newcomers rather than seeking opportunities for engagement and learning.

Organisation studies and complexity theory provide useful insights into the important functions played by network-type linkages in helping complex systems to manage themselves within turbulent (ever-changing) environments. Complex systems that are sufficiently well connected demonstrate a tendency to 'self-organise' over time, with clusters and groups emerging from the pattern of interactions among the participating 'members'. In some cases these configurations evolve as formal structures that survive so long as they fit a niche in the organisational environment. Network modes of organising are said to reduce transaction costs, though in reality these are simply transferred to less public arenas, where invisible emotional work builds trust and mutuality. Networks operate as highly effective communication channels, gathering intelligence from a range of sources and processing it to become collective wisdom or 'common sense'. Community networks convey information and ideas, recruiting potential collaborators and supporters for self-help groups and collective action.

Communities can be thought of as complex systems comprising overlapping networks of social and organisational relationships. Their boundaries are difficult to define; they consist of multiple, interdependent elements; there exists no centralised control mechanism; and interactions between members are governed by localised and relatively simple conventions. Well-functioning communities possess a range of capacities for absorbing or adapting to change, managing internal tensions and generating (and dissolving) a variety of forms for collective action.

These capacities are organic and 'owned' by communities them-selves. In many instances, they has been built up over years of collective action among a fairly stable population who accumulate skills, knowledge and confidence from a shared experience of successful organising. Social networks with diverse, boundary-spanning contacts are particularly useful, especially where these provide links to other communities and powerful agencies. Loose networks are often the precursors to more formal organisational arrangements, especially where these involve people or organisations from a diversity of backgrounds and interests.

Social movements depend on activist networks to organise collective action, to raise awareness and to lobby for change. For example, the first Bristol Festival Against Racism was organised entirely through the political, professional and personal networks of the main coordinators. Having no resources of its own, it used connections to mobilise organisations, galvanise individuals, generate ideas, gain access to funding and distribute its publicity. Trust and shared values were vital to these achievements and the organisers particularly encouraged groups to work together where there had previously been only limited contact. A subsequent evaluation of the initiative revealed that participation in the Festival had reinforced people's commitment and confidence around anti-racism. A framework had been established on which stronger, more diverse networks could grow. The success of the Festival Against Racism provided a model for subsequent RESPECT events and has important implications for strategies to develop greater community cohesion.

However, some areas and some sections of the population lack what has been termed 'community capacity' and are disadvantaged as a result. Informal networks might be cliquey, perpetuating power imbalances and fostering segregation rather than integration across different groups. Consequently, such communities find it difficult to represent their interests to public decision-making bodies and react to conflict and crises in ways that are seen by outsiders as chaotic or apathetic.

Networking for community development

Tackling such situations involves strategic and well-resourced interventions, including support for individuals who take on representative or leadership roles, and help with setting up and managing formal organisations.

Community development has traditionally emphasised these two approaches, now the focus of several government initiatives, for example, Community Champions and FutureBuilders. While these are making important contributions to strengthening voluntary and community sector capacity, they are not the most effective means of building social capital.

Community development has been defined as '[being] about building active and sustainable communities based on social justice and mutual respect. It is about changing power structures to remove barriers that prevent people from participating in the issues that affect their lives'.[6] A vital, but underestimated aspect of this work is the practical, psychological and political support that nurtures informal networks. Community workers often find themselves acting as interpreters and mediators within communities, helping people to talk and work together when there are difficulties relating to language, assumptions and the occasional antagonism. They may themselves provide the 'boundary-spanning mechanisms', brokering joint ventures between organisations or staying in touch through informal conversation.

Ideally, effort and resources should be used to create the conditions where communities can grow and maintain their own networks, recognising that extra guidance and assistance may be needed to ensure that these are inclusive, diverse and extrovert. This means helping with the boundary-spanning connections and addressing power differentials and obstacles to effective cooperation. There are many ways in which community development activities can encourage and enhance networking. Indeed this is a core purpose for community development.[7] Community workers provide contact details and information for the communities they work with and other practitioners. They direct people to appropriate agencies or funding bodies. Community workers work with communities to arrange activities such as street festivals or meetings, where networking happens fairly naturally, though they may have a role in ensuring that such events are fully accessible to all members of the relevant communities. Communal buildings such as community centres or village halls provide space for casual interaction as well as more purposeful joint working. These need to be safe, welcoming and affordable, so the décor, location and publicity may need careful consideration to avoid the space being dominated by certain groups. Experience suggests that this will require continuous monitoring and occasional interventions to deal with inevitable conflicts and misunderstandings.

Conclusion

The idea of the well-connected community should not be seen as a nostalgic, communitarian model of urban neighbourhoods or village life. It is a radical approach that celebrates the dynamic and multi-faceted nature of our lives while asserting the value of social connectivity. Community development strategies that strengthen and extend informal networks are essential to tackling social exclusion and building community cohesion. They improve and sustain partnership working by building trust between partners and ensuring more representative community involvement. These processes are not amenable to the current audit regimes of targets and indicators, and progress is better measured using techniques of participatory appraisal and network analysis. It is difficult to predict, let alone control, outcomes and it is therefore likely that this model will be resisted by policy-makers and politicians who are interested in tangible and short-term gains. However, if the rhetoric of civil renewal and community-led regeneration are to be translated into real changes in people's lives, then informal networks, supported where necessary by community workers, are crucial components of the journey towards a fairer, more sustainable vision of social justice.

Alison Gilchrist is Director of Practice Development at the Community Development Foundation and the author of The Well-connected Community: a networking approach to community development.

Notes

1   G Chanan, *Searching for Solid Foundations: community involvement and urban policy* (London: ODPM, 2003).

2   M Mayo and M Taylor, 'Partnership and power in community regeneration' in S Balloch and M Taylor (eds), *Partnership Working* (Bristol: Policy Press, 2001).

3   R Putnam, *Bowling Alone: the collapse and revival of American community* (New York: Simon and Shuster, 2000).

4   See for example, P Walker et al, *Prove It: measuring the effect of neighbourhood renewal on local people* (London: New Economics Foundation, 2000) and Bassac's BEDE programme, available at www.bassac.org.uk/info_bede.htm.

5   F Capra, *The Web of Life: a new synthesis of mind and matter* (London: HarperCollins, 1996).

6   Standing Conference for Community Development, *Strategic Framework for Community Development* (Sheffield: SCCD, 2001).

7   A Gilchrist, 'The well-connected community: networking to the "edge of chaos"', *Community Development Journal* 35 (2000).

Not all networks are created equal. The mistake has been to equate their existence with mechanisms of effective social action . . .

Networks and neighbourhoods

Robert J Sampson

DEM☺S

12. Networks and neighbourhoods

the implications of connectivity for thinking about crime in the modern city

Robert J Sampson

The idyllic notion of local communities as 'urban villages' characterised by dense networks of personal ties is a seductive image, and one that pervades theoretical perspectives on neighbourhood crime. The idea seems to be that tight-knit neighbourhoods are safe because of their rich supply of social networks. Yet such ideal typical neighbourhoods appear to bear little resemblance to contemporary cities where weak ties prevail over strong ties and social interaction among residents is characterised more by instrumentality than altruism. Moreover, the dark side of 'community' is often neglected – social networks can and often are put to use for illegal or violent purposes. In short, a deceptive conflation of networks and neighbourhoods characterises the current scene.

The urban village model of cities is further compromised by the assumption that networks of personal ties map neatly on to the geographically defined boundaries of neighbourhoods, such that neighbourhoods can be analysed as independent social entities. In fact, social networks in the modern city frequently traverse traditional ecological boundaries, many of which are permeable and vaguely defined. Living in close proximity to high-crime neighbourhoods may increase the risk of crime no matter what the density of social networks in an adjacent neighbourhood. It follows that neighbourhoods themselves need to be conceptualised as nodes in a larger network of spatial relations.

In this essay I explore these issues by considering new ways of thinking about the relevance of neighbourhoods and networks that nonetheless build on important work of the past. Tradition needs to be transcended, not discarded. Neighbourhoods, after all, show remarkable continuities in patterns of criminal activity. For at least a hundred years criminological research in the ecological tradition has confirmed the concentration of interpersonal violence in certain neighbourhoods, especially those characterised by poverty, the racial segregation of minority groups, and the concentration of single-parent families. The challenge, then, is to incorporate new urban realities into our understanding of crime – and ultimately our policy responses.

From social disorganisation to networks

The intellectual history of situating social networks in local neighbourhoods is a venerable one. In the classic work of the Chicago School of Urban Sociology in the early twentieth century it was thought that density, low economic status, ethnic heterogeneity and residential instability led to the rupture of local social ties, which in turn accounted for high rates of crime and disorder. Later in the century, the concept of social disorganisation came to be defined as the inability of a community to realise the common values of its residents and maintain effective social order. This theoretical definition was formulated in systemic terms – the allegedly disorganised community was viewed as suffering from a disrupted or weakened system of friendship, kinship and acquaintanceship networks, and thus ultimately of processes of socialisation.

More recently, the intellectual tradition of community-level research has been revitalised by the increasingly popular idea of 'social capital'. Although there are conflicting definitions, social capital is typically conceptualised as being embodied in the social ties among persons. In an influential version, Robert Putnam defines social capital as the networks, norms, and trust that facilitate coordination and cooperation for mutual benefit.[1] The connection of social disorganisation and social capital theory can be articulated as follows: neighbourhoods bereft of social capital (read social networks) are less able to realise common values and maintain the social controls that foster safety.

Despite the popular appeal of social capital, there are good reasons to question the translation of strong social ties into low crime rates. First, in some neighbourhood contexts strong ties may impede efforts to establish social control. William Julius Wilson, for example, has argued that residents of very poor neighbourhoods tend to be tightly interconnected through network ties but without necessarily producing collective resources such as social control. He reasons that ties in the inner city are excessively personalistic and parochial in nature – socially isolated from public resources.[2]

Second, networks connect do-gooders just as they connect drug dealers. In her study of a black middle-class community in Chicago, Pattillo-McCoy specifically addresses the limits of tight-knit social bonds in facilitating social control.[3] She argues that although dense local ties do promote social cohesion, at the same time they foster the growth of networks that impede efforts to rid the neighbourhood of organised drug- and gang-related crime. In this way, dense social ties have both positive and negative repercussions, reminding us that in a consideration of networks it is important to ask *what* is being connected – networks are not inherently egalitarian or prosocial in nature.

Third, shared expectations for social control and strategic connections that yield action can be fostered in the absence of thick ties among neighbours. As Granovetter argued in his seminal essay, 'weak ties'– less intimate connections between people based on more infrequent social interaction – may be critical for establishing social resources, such as job referrals, because they integrate the community by way of bringing together otherwise disconnected subgroups.[4] Consistent with this view, there is evidence that weak ties among neighbours, as manifested in middle-range rather than either non-existent or intensive social interaction, are predictive of lower crime rates.

Collective efficacy

Research on dense social ties reveals a paradox of sorts for thinking about crime. Many city-dwellers have only limited interaction with their neighbours and yet appear to generate community-specific social capital. Moreover, urban areas where strong ties are tightly restricted geographically may actually produce a climate that discourages collective responses to local problems. To address these urban realities, in recent work I and my colleagues have proposed a focus on mechanisms of social control that may be facilitated by, but do not necessarily require, strong ties or associations.[5] Rejecting the outmoded assumption that neighbourhoods are characterised by dense, intimate, emotional bonds, I define neighbourhoods in ecological terms and highlight variations in the working trust and shared willingness of residents to intervene in achieving social control. The concept of neighbourhood 'collective efficacy' captures the importance of this link between trust and cohesion on the one hand and shared expectations for control on the other. Just as self-efficacy is situated rather than general (one has self-efficacy relative to a particular task), a neighbourhood's efficacy exists relative to specific tasks such as maintaining public order.

Viewed through this theoretical lens, collective efficacy is a task-specific construct that draws attention to shared expectations and mutual engagement by residents in local social control. To measure the social control aspect of collective efficacy, we have asked residents about the likelihood that their neighbours could be counted on to take action under various scenarios (for example, children skipping school and hanging out on a street corner, or the fire station closest to home being threatened with budget cuts). The cohesion and working trust dimension has been measured by items that capture the extent of local trust, willingness to help neighbours, a close-knit fabric, lack of conflict and shared values. Published results show that after controlling for a range of individual and neighbourhood charac-teristics, including poverty and the density of friendship ties, *collective efficacy is associated with lower rates of violence*. Neighbourhoods high in collective efficacy predict significantly lower rates of violence even where earlier experience of violence may have depressed collective efficacy because of fear.

Moving away from a focus on private ties, use of the term 'collective efficacy' is meant to signify an emphasis on shared beliefs in a neighbourhood's capability for action to achieve an intended effect, coupled with an active sense of engagement on the part of residents. Some density of social networks is essential, to be sure, especially networks rooted in social trust. But the key theoretical point is that *networks have to be activated to be ultimately meaningful.* Collective efficacy therefore helps to elevate the 'agentic' aspect of social life over a perspective centred on the accumulation of stocks of social resources (or what some call 'social capital'). This is consistent with a redefinition of social capital in terms of expectations for action within a collectivity.

Distinguishing between the resource potential represented by personal ties, on the one hand, and the shared expectations for action among neighbours represented by collective efficacy, on the other, helps clarify the dense networks paradox: *social networks foster the conditions under which collective efficacy may flourish, but they are not sufficient for the exercise of control.* So the theoretical framework proposed here recognises the transformed landscape of modern urban life, holding that while community efficacy may depend on working trust and social interaction, it does not require that my neighbour or the local police officer be my friend.

Exclusive and non-exclusive social networks

As noted above, recent writing on social capital tends to gloss over its potential downside – namely that social capital can be drawn upon for negative as well as positive goals. After all, resources can be put to many uses, and therefore some constraints on goals are theoretically necessary. For example, we would not consider racial exclusion, as practised in many a 'defended' neighbourhood, to be a desirable result of networking. Many neighbourhood associations in American cities have been so exploited by whites to keep blacks from moving to white working-class areas. Although often resisted by social scientists,

I therefore believe there is a need to invoke a normative or goal-directed dimension when evaluating social networks and collective efficacy.

To judge whether neighbourhood structures serve collective needs I apply the 'non-exclusivity requirement' of a social good – does its consumption by one member of a community diminish the sum available to the community as a whole? For example, I would argue that safety, clean environments, quality education for children, active maintenance of intergenerational ties, the reciprocal exchange of information and services among families, and the shared willingness to intervene on behalf of the neighbourhood all produce a social good that yields positive 'externalities' potentially of benefit to all residents – especially children. As with other resources that produce positive externalities, I believe that collective efficacy is widely desired but much harder to achieve, owing in large part to structural constraints. Ultimately, then, I view the role of social networks in the production of collective efficacy not as a simple panacea but as dependent on specific normative and structural contexts.

The natural question that follows is: what are the kinds of contexts that promote collective efficacy and non-exclusive social networks? Although it is beyond the scope of this essay, I would argue that the infrastructure and cohesion of organisations help sustain capacity for social action in a way that transcends traditional personal ties. In other words, organisations are at least in principle able to foster collective efficacy, often through strategic networking of their own. Whether garbage removal, choosing the site of a fire station, school improvements, or police responses, a continuous stream of challenges faces modern communities, challenges that no longer can be met (if they ever were) by relying solely on individuals. Action depends on connections among organisations, connections that are not necessarily dense or reflective of the structure of personal ties in a neighbourhood. Our research supports this position, showing that the density of local organisations and voluntary associations predicts higher levels of collective efficacy, controlling for poverty and the social composition of the population.[6]

Figure 1 Neighbourhood inequality, social processes and safety

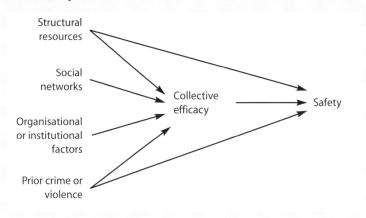

Inequality in other resources nonetheless still matters for explaining the production of collective efficacy. Concentrated disadvantage and lack of home ownership, for example, predict lower levels of later collective efficacy, and the associations of disadvantage and housing instability with violence are significantly reduced when collective efficacy is controlled. These patterns are consistent with the inference that neighbourhood constraints influence violence in part through the mediating role of neighbourhood efficacy. Our work suggests that social resources and social networks create the capacity for collective efficacy, but it is the act of exercising control under conditions of trust that is the most proximate to explaining crime (see Figure 1).

Spatial networks

Networks need not be conceptualised only in personal terms. I would argue that neighbourhoods are themselves nodes in a larger network of spatial relations. Contrary to the common assumption in criminology of analytic independence, my contention is that neighbourhoods are interdependent and characterised by a functional relationship between what happens at one point in space and what happens elsewhere.

Consider first the inexact correspondence between the neighbourhood boundaries imposed by census geography and the ecological properties that shape social interaction. One of the biggest criticisms of neighbourhood-level research to date concerns the artificiality of boundaries; for example, two families living across the street from one another may be arbitrarily assigned to live in different 'neighbourhoods' even though they share social ties. From the standpoint of systemic theory, it is thus important to account for social and institutional ties that link residents across neighbourhoods. The idea of spatial dependence challenges the urban village model, which implicitly assumes that neighbourhoods represent intact social systems, functioning as islands unto themselves.

Second, spatial dependence is implicated by the fact that offenders are disproportionately involved in acts of violence near their homes. From a routine activities perspective, it follows that a neighbourhood's risk of violence is heightened by geographical proximity to places where known offenders live or to places characterised by risk factors such as concentrated poverty or low collective efficacy.

A third motivation for studying spatial dependence relates to the notion that interpersonal crimes such as homicide are based on social interaction and thus subject to processes of diffusion – where knock-on effects may be felt far from the initial point of impact. Acts of violence may themselves instigate a sequence of events that leads to further violence in a spatially channelled way. A key insight, for example, is that many homicides are retaliatory in nature, such that a homicide in one neighbourhood may provide the spark that eventually leads to a retaliatory killing in a nearby neighbourhood. In addition, most homicides occur among persons known to one another, usually involving networks of association that follow a geographical logic.

There are good reasons, then, to believe that the characteristics of surrounding neighbourhoods are crucial to understanding violence in any given neighbourhood. Our findings support this notion by establishing the salience of spatial proximity and the inequality of neighbourhood resources that are played out in citywide dynamics. The mechanisms of racial segregation reinforce spatial inequality, explaining why it is, for example, that despite similar income profiles black middle-class neighbourhoods are at greater risk of violence than white middle-class neighbourhoods. In short, violence is conditioned by the characteristics of spatially proximate neighbourhoods, which in turn are conditioned by adjoining neighbourhoods in a spatially linked process that ultimately characterises the entire metropolitan system. Policies that focus solely on the internal characteristics of neighbourhoods, as is typical, are simply insufficient.

Conclusion

We live in a network society, or so we are widely told. But not all networks are created equal, and many lie dormant. The mistake has been to equate the existence of networks with mechanisms of effective social action. As Arthur Stinchcombe put it in a useful analogy, just as road systems have their causal impact through the flow of traffic, so systems of links among people and organisations (and in our case, neighbourhoods) have their causal impact through what flows through them.[7] The problem then becomes obvious – through neighbourhood networks flows the full spectrum of life's realities, whether despair, criminal knowledge, friendship or social control.

In this essay I have considered one small slice of the problem. My basic position is that collective action for problem-solving is a crucial causal mechanism that is differentially activated under specific kinds of contextual conditions. The density of social networks is only one and probably not the most important characteristic of neighbourhoods that contributes to effective social action. I have also argued that neighbourhoods themselves are part of a spatial network encompassing the entire city. To use an overworked term, not only are individuals embedded, so too are neighbourhoods.

Nothing in the logic of my approach is limited to the United States, or any country for that matter. Our current research is seeking to examine the role of spatial inequality and neighbourhood efficacy in several cities around the world. To date we have explored a neighbourhood-level, cross-national comparison of Chicago and Stockholm. Although Chicago and Stockholm vary dramatically in their social structure and levels of violence, this does not necessarily imply a difference in the processes or mechanisms that link communities and crime. Indeed, our analyses suggest that rates of violence are predicted by collective efficacy in Stockholm as in Chicago. Furthermore, collective efficacy is promoted by housing stability and undermined by concentrated disadvantage – again similarly in both cities and in accord with our general theory. The data are thus consistent with a general approach to social policy that emphasises ameliorating neighbourhood inequality in social resources and enhancing social conditions that foster the collective efficacy of residents and organisations.

Robert Sampson is Henry Ford II Professor of the Social Sciences at Harvard University.

Notes

1   R Putnam, 'The prosperous community: social capital and community life', *American Prospect*, Spring (1993).
2   WJ Wilson, *The Truly Disadvantaged* (Chicago: University of Chicago Press, 1978).
3   ME Pattillo-McCoy, *Black Picket Fences: privilege and peril among the black middle class* (Chicago: University of Chicago Press, 1999).
4   MS Granovetter, 'The strength of weak ties', *American Journal of Sociology* 78 (1973).
5   RJ Sampson, SW Raudenbush and F Earls, 'Neighborhoods and violent crime: a multilevel study of collective efficacy', *Science* 277 (1997).
6   J Morenoff, RJ Sampson, SW Raudenbush, 'Neighborhood inequality, collective efficacy, and the spatial dynamics of urban violence', *Criminology* 39 (2001).
7   A Stinchcombe, 'An outsider's view of network analyses of power' in R Perrucci and H Potter, *Networks of Power* (New York: Aldine De Gruyter, 1989).

Delegating judgement and individualising service would be a radical departure for most of the private and all of the public sector …

Organising for success

Diane Coyle

DEM⊙S

13. Organising for success

how network technologies are changing organisations

Diane Coyle

Swimming in the vast tides of information that are the result of new(ish) network technologies it is easy to overlook a simple consequence of cheap communications and information processing. There is more of both, of course – none of us could miss that. But all that information is also flowing into different places. It isn't a question of having the same connections as before, only faster: entirely new connections are developing.

That is easy enough to understand in the abstract. What does it mean in a specific context, such as a particular company or public sector agency? Organisations take the shape they have for many reasons, including historical accidents, political outcomes and cultural context. However, one key explanation for organisational structure is the ease or difficulty of exchanging information. The reason companies exist is because there are compelling reasons for some transactions not to take place in a market between individuals. An important one is the existence of economies of scale. But others concern the lack of information: the difficulty of monitoring quality and effort or the impossibility of writing down all possible contingencies in a watertight contract. In addition, companies take certain internal forms because of problems like monitoring workers' productivity or keeping track of the large amount of information relevant to day-to-day decisions.

If it is costly and difficult to exchange information, companies are more likely to be large, composed of many internal businesses, and hierarchical. It will make sense to integrate essential supplies and services in one single organisation. And it will make sense to channel relevant information up a pyramid and have a set of rules for which decisions need to be taken at each level of the business. Conversely, if information flows more easily, outsourcing, breaking up conglomerates and flattening hierarchies will look more attractive.

And so it is been since the early 1990s, when the steep recession triggered a substantial corporate reorganisation with exactly these features. Although they might have looked like straightforward cost-cutting or management fads, each had a fundamental technological rationale.

The pattern throughout the past decade has been a hollowing-out of medium-sized companies. A huge merger wave created more very big companies, increasingly with an internal network rather than a hierarchical structure, taking advantage of economies of scale and global market opportunities. The possibilities of ICT have allowed more small companies to thrive by exploiting better and faster information on specialist consumer demands or specialised sources of supply, and operating in an external network of other companies. The relative advantages of being in between have diminished. Indeed, being medium-sized can combine all the disadvantages of lacking scale with all the disadvantages of lacking flexibility.

There are no consistent data across countries, but the OECD has estimated from different national sources that the average size of companies has been shrinking. The number employing more than 500 people has declined since 1990 – although the remaining big companies are almost certainly much bigger than before. And in most industrial countries (Japan being a significant exception) the number of businesses employing up to 50 people has rocketed.[1]

It is hard to be sure how far this size redistribution will go, for there will certainly always be some big firms around. But it is a safe bet that the organisational and social ramifications are still in their infancy.

Electricity and the flow of production

The radical possibilities new technologies might hold for the organisational shape of British business are easier to appreciate from a past example. Just how far can organisational change resulting from a new technology actually go?

Take the case of electrification following the invention of the electric dynamo in 1870. This innovation made it possible to run every machine in a factory from a separate electric motor, rather than all machines running from a single energy source, a steam engine. In the latter case, all the machines had to be clustered around a central drive shaft, so factories and mills were built on several storeys. If one needed to be shut down for repair or maintenance, the whole factory stopped. With an electric motor on each machine, they could be halted individually and arranged in any order.

In fact, the machines could be much more efficiently laid out on one storey according to the logical sequence of production – at least, once new factories were being built. Single-storey buildings could have more windows – even in the roof – which increased productivity further, and also improved safety. And once managers and engineers started to think about altering the pattern of production, the way was open for the assembly line.

The ramifications of the dynamo can be traced back further still. Whereas factories used to be in town centres, the advantages of flat, low buildings – along with concerns about urban conditions – created an impetus towards building on greenfield suburban sites. Housing followed the jobs, although of course the internal combustion engine played a more central role in the development of suburbs and urban sprawl.

The new style of factory needed machine operatives performing more standardised tasks, the more so as the pattern of production increasingly took on assembly line form. So instead of craft skills, the demand was for a basic standard education. This in turn encouraged the development of public primary and secondary schools, batch-producing assembly line workers. It is not too fanciful to see the culmination of the cluster of new technologies based on the electric motor, developed in the late nineteenth century and diffused during the early twentieth century, as culminating in the Fordist model of production and mass consumer society.

The economies of scale and high initial capital requirements for these mass-production plants favoured the emergence of very large conglomerate companies. The early part of the twentieth century saw a period of dramatic industrial consolidation, with the number of firms in most industries shrinking from the hundreds to the handfuls – most dramatically in the automobile and electrical goods industries themselves.

Today's new technologies and the flow of service

It would be an exaggeration to say that these earlier forces shaping corporate organisation have been swept away. On the contrary, economies of scale are more important than ever in many significant industries – more important because if they can be exploited on a global scale they can give a business a near impregnable competitive advantage. And more important too because of the network externalities or initial research and development costs involved in many important new goods – consider software or biotech products. In these cases spending on research and development is a kind of strategic arms race in which it is getting harder and harder for new competitors to enter the business. Big is definitely better in these cases.

On the other hand, new opportunities are opening up due to the fragmentation of demand. There has been an explosion in the choice offered to consumers thanks to the increased flow of information. Consumers are better able to communicate their specific preferences to companies. Companies are better able to collect and act on that information, through improved logistics and vastly more flexible networked production systems.

Nobody ever thought quantity was the spice of life. When our basic needs are met, we seek to meet additional wants in varied ways. So we have seen in recent years an explosion in quality and variety. Henry

Ford famously said of the Model T: 'The customer can have any colour he wants so long as it is black.' The choice of new vehicle models in US is now nearly 300; Ford offers 46 colours. The paradigm now isn't Ford but Dell. It gives customers who order online 16 million theoretical combinations of specifications for a desktop PC.

Amazon has 2.3 million books available compared with 250,000 in the biggest New York book superstore, and 40,000 to 100,000 in most big bookstores. Nearly half the books ordered from Amazon.com are titles not likely to be in stock in any physical store. In addition the ability to search for titles and discover books online has also increased special orders through physical stores by an unknown amount. MIT Press estimates that online discovery has helped increase orders for its backlist titles by 12 per cent. These spillovers, increasing market size, improve the viability of publishing titles for a non-mass readership and further increase variety in a virtuous circle. MIT economist Erik Brynjolfsson estimates that the welfare gain to American consumers from being able to choose books not available in stock in big bookstores at about \$1 billion a year, roughly five times the biggest estimates of gains from lower prices online.[2]

Within this massively expanded array of choice in all kinds of products, from toothpaste to computers, there are many niche markets in which relatively small companies can compete effectively. Even where they are selling tangible products, they are adding value essentially through providing a service. The service can be thought of as information-broking – or more creatively as the satisfaction of desires, the desires of individuals to step outside the mass market and craft themselves.

This is a product of the fact that value added in the advanced economies is increasingly weightless (literally so – UK GDP weighed roughly the same in 1999 as in 1990, although it had grown by a quarter in real terms, according to the ONS).[3] The way companies can attract customers is through the service-like elements of what they sell, not through processing stuff.

The essence of service is customisation – something one person does for another. While there's plenty of scope for standardisation in many sectors we categorise as services, such as processing insurance claims or sorting cheques, these are low-value activities. Value added in service and manufacturing sectors alike lies more and more in individualisation, not standardisation.

Ultimately that means a transaction between individual customers and individual employees, using the vastly increased flow of information available to both. For all the hype about employee empowerment and being a 'people business', very few companies have delegated genuine decision-making authority to the level of the individual employee. The parameters for making judgements without referring up what's left of the hierarchy are usually tightly circumscribed.

Implications

Delegating real judgement to permit individualised service would be a radical departure from the organisational forms prevalent in most private businesses and all of the public sector today. Indeed, public services are still in the Model T Ford era, and the debate on 'standards' – the adjective 'high' is implicit – indicates that nobody is really thinking beyond standardisation. Yet many people are unlikely to be satisfied for much longer with the Fordist model as citizens when as consumers they are increasingly offered the Dell model. And as consumers they are also increasingly dissatisfied with, say, a standard call-centre script. They want an individual response. The information is available to permit it – it is the organisational form that lags behind.

And understandably so, for this kind of radical organisational devolution demands a high level of mutual trust between employees and managers – and ultimately investors and owners. Remember, the transactions that take place within organisations are those it is too difficult to transact in a market because of the informational constraints. Yet it is extremely difficult to monitor the productivity and quality of a non-standard service inside an organisation too. The companies that add the most value will be the ones with the highest levels of internal trust.

This is a profound management challenge. In theory, the new information and communications technologies permit any employee of a business to have real-time access to all kinds of information that would allow her or him to make better – more profitable – decisions. But very few companies indeed take advantage of this possibility. The evidence is, though, that all the productivity gains from the technologies are concentrated among companies that have undergone organisational change. No change, no gain – but if work is reorganised, the level of productivity in the business can jump by 25 or 30 per cent according to case study evidence.[4] Such figures are a measure of how much consumers are willing to pay for improved quality and customisation.

The transition from the type of company and employment relationship we have now to the type suggested by the logic of a free-information world is going to be at least as radical – and as slow – as the shift from Victorian entrepreneurialism to 1950s corporatism. And yet the logic is there. With the average company life now down to under 20 years, any business that can trace its roots back to the nineteenth century and which hopes to survive through the twenty-first century should start struggling with it now.

Diane Coyle runs Enlightenment Economics and is a visiting professor at Manchester University's Institute for Political and Economic Governance. She is the author of, among other books, Paradoxes of Prosperity *and* The Weightless World.

Notes

1   B van Ark and E Monnikhof, 'Size distribution of output and employment: a data set for five OECD countries 1960s–1990', Economics Department Working Paper no 166 (Paris: OECD, 1996).
2   E Brynjolfsson, MD Smith and Y Hu, 'Consumer surplus in the digital economy: estimating the value of increased product variety at online booksellers', MIT Working Paper, April (2003).
3   C Sheerin, 'UK material flow accounting', *Economic Trends* 583, June (2002).
4   See, for example, T Bresnahan, E Brynjolfsson and L Hitt, 'IT, workplace organisation and the demand for skilled labor: a firm-level analysis', MIT Working Paper (2002); E Brynjolfsson and L Hitt, 'Paradox lost? Firm-level

evidence on the return to information systems spending', *Management Science*, 42 no 4 (1997); E Brynjolfsson and L Hitt, 'Computing productivity: are computers pulling their weight?', MIT Working Paper (2000); E Brynjolfsson and L Hitt, 'Beyond computation: information technology and organisational transformation', *Journal of Economic Perspectives* 14 no 4, Fall (2000); McKinsey Global Institute, *US Productivity Growth 1995–2000: understanding the impact of information technology relative to other factors*, October (2001).

Smart devices will be worn in your clothing, jewellery and accessories, and will hop in to local wireless networks when they need to . . .

The information utility

John Taylor

DEM☉S

14. The information utility

John Taylor

We are entering the era of the information utility. Billions of computers, smart devices and huge data resources are inexorably becoming society's indispensable infrastructure. Information utilities are set to become as pervasive as printing, electricity, the automobile and telephone – and just as disruptive to existing social practices and forms of organisation. Futurologists have produced innumerable accounts of the importance of electronic networks such as the internet in shaping our world. Social and management scientists have written similarly about the importance of social networks of human beings in characterising all aspects of society. From now on 'networking' means an intimate combination of the two: people and technology.

It is helpful to think of the information utility as comprising what goes on 'behind the wall', what is 'in front of the wall', and crucially the two-way interactions that can go on 'through the wall' between people and things connected to the utility. Behind the wall there will be huge amounts of connectivity, computing power and data resources of all kinds. When you access the information utility from any location in the world you will not have to worry about where the resources are or how they work, any more than you worry about where the electricity and water come from when you turn on your dishwasher. In front of the wall, there will be billions of smart devices of all kinds connected wirelessly to each other and to the utility, enabling billions of people to be online all the time they want to be.

These sets of information utilities evolving around the world represent an emerging 'global information infrastructure'. What makes this emergence possible – indeed, inevitable – is partly the continuing pace of technological change: Moore's law will still enable the underlying microelectronics technology to deliver a doubling of price-performance every 18 months for the next 10–20 years; storage technology – hard discs, CDs, flash memory and so on – is getting cheaper even faster than this, with really disruptive new technologies in the pipeline such as atomic resolution storage and holographic memory. But it is also the result of the demand-side pressures unleashed by the new and radical capabilities that this infrastructure will possess, and the useful (or simply delightful) applications to which they may be put.

Behind the wall

We are already seeing the first generation of the worldwide information utility in the form of e-science Grids building on the internet and the World Wide Web. Already today's internet and telecommunications infrastructure probably comprises at least ten billion computers and 100 exabytes (100 billion billion bytes) of data. At least 600 million people can currently access the internet, which carries about 4 billion emails per day, and between 1 and 2 billion people worldwide now have phones.

The information utility will be qualitatively unlike any previous global communication system such as road, rail, air or telephone networks. It will consist of huge amounts of interconnected data and computing power, and it will be able to interact through the wall with tens of billions of smart devices of all kinds, and through them with billions of people. In this way it will progressively exhibit more and more 'intelligence'. We are already seeing the rise of 'intelligent' software and machine learning, as the ability of humans to design and programme large systems reaches its limits. The rich interconnection between elements of the infrastructure will mean that a software object that turns out to be powerful and useful for some particular task will be able to replicate, spread and 'jump species' around the infrastructure in many fewer 'generations' than we see in biological systems. Evolution through incremental enhancement and (often unpredictable) adaptation will become a key paradigm.

We have already reached the stage when the global communications infrastructure can no longer be thought of as 'a system' in the traditional, hard engineering sense of the word. It has no specification. It was not designed by any one person or organisation, nor is it implemented, owned, operated or maintained by any recognisable single authority. It is never the same from one access to the next so faults cannot be reproduced. The underlying engineering principles and protocols are based on having to know as little as possible about what is going on in the infrastructure, rather than knowing as much as possible; the old IT tradition of 'full documentation' is long gone. Instead it may be more appropriate to think of the utility as a system in the biological sense of a living, complex, adaptive whole, continuously evolving through the collaboration of many autonomous subsystems.

A crucial property of such large sets of cooperating elements is that they collectively display 'emergent behaviour', which is not readily predictable from a knowledge of the individual elements. Emergent behaviours come from systems involving decision-making entities, like the way ant colonies organise their collective activities to discover and retrieve food. An emergent behaviour involving the internet itself is spamming. About 50 per cent of all the email on the internet this year is spam, up from 2 per cent a couple of years ago.

In front of the wall

Our understanding of emergent behaviours in complex systems is still very primitive, but will have to become highly sophisticated if we are to grasp the full implications of the world of the information utility, a world populated not just by billions of people and smart things but also by a huge cloud of 'agents' of many different kinds. Some of these will be designed to make our lives easier by mediating our interactions with the infrastructure, carrying out tasks and negotiating with other agents. Sometimes these entities may take on 'personalities' that engage in natural dialogue with people, and will have the ability to evolve, adapt and learn.

These agents will be enabled by the billions of smart devices linked through wireless networks to the utility and sometimes each other. These devices will be able to form 'ad hoc' networks that come together for a specific, temporary purpose. For example, several cars in proximity may want to talk to each other to avoid having a potential crash on a particular stretch of road; a group of people who have come together for a meeting may want their agents to set up arrangements for them to work together on a set of documents and presentations; a shopper may want to interact with specific products in the supermarket he or she happens to be in. Smart devices will be worn in your clothing, jewellery and accessories, and hop into the utility via local wireless networks whenever they need to.

Any thing that uses power today will use the information utility tomorrow. Any thing can be made smart and networked, and its physical location and status tracked using location services such as Global Positioning System (GPS) and cellphone networks, satellite imaging and tagging technologies like Radio Frequency Identification (RFID) tags. We already know how to keep track of millions, often billions, of people, animals, vehicles, personal belongings, electrical appliances and household objects. We can't (yet) cope with trillions of trillions of insects, weeds, birds, leaves, flowers, rocks or stones. But vast digital archive networks are now burgeoning into existence with every conceivable kind of information, from molecular structures and astronomical observatories to records of individuals' genetic material, their medical histories, financial transactions and electronic communications.

And the infrastructure can also be connected to a huge range of instruments and devices, from earth surveillance satellites that monitor crops, water and weather, to CCTV cameras, webcams and astronomical telescopes. These, and many others, offer real-time data to users, acting as the eyes, ears and sensors of the global infrastructure. In a very practicable sense this will support the instrumentation of the planet in a wholly unprecedented way. It will become very hard for countries and companies to keep most of their activities from being visible in detail and in real time to the rest of the world.

Through the wall

Perhaps the most subtle and far-reaching impact of the information utility will be its ability to support and mediate interactions between people through the wall. Today, accessing a web page is a solitary activity undertaken between a person and a website. Teleconferencing and videoconferencing remain primitive and cumbersome, and 'personal networks' among people get very little support from ICTs beyond phones and email.

One of the key advances of the information utility will therefore be to support fluent collaboration and cooperation between groups and teams of people: at work, socially, in families, at play. These collaborative environments – or *col-laboratories* – will be the infrastructure for teams of knowledge workers and citizens who trust each other to work together to create new intellectual property or social goods. It will be invaluable for lawyers working on a case, say, or for a design team working on a new product. It will also be ideal for supporting outsourcing and collaboration between companies and organisations – for example, where a contract requires people from several organisations to work securely together for a limited period of time.

The signs that this is already happening are with us. Each year we are becoming more dependent on an extremely complex interconnected infrastructure, which supports more and more of our everyday lives. This dependence is becoming crucial and irreversible. Gradually we will be more and more unable to function without it. It is instructive to look at a few examples.

Work

E-business and the continued development of outsourcing already demand unprecedented levels of dynamic, fleet-of-foot inter-firm collaborations. The advent of secure collaborative environments will accelerate the ability of people to work as individuals in several different teams and companies, and for companies to have temporary, and often casual and exploratory relationships with each other.

This will drive the need for new business models, audit practices and concepts of intellectual property (IP). If a new animated movie or commercial is created by an ad hoc collaboration of people using fragments of pre-existing characters, personalities, story lines, music and synthetic locations obtained from sources in the utility and added to by the creative work of the team, then who should get paid for what? We will need new systems for tracking, banking and remunerating knowledge work. There may be a need for new forms of micro-IP and micro-payments, with audit trails trusted by the various participants.

Education and learning

The students and knowledge workers of tomorrow will be permanently and wirelessly online to the information utility and each other. In place of textbooks and ringbinders of notes, each person will build up a lifelong personal information space comprising millions of personal items and millions of persistent reliable links to web pages, other information resources and other people. Accessing these resources casually and continually as a matter of course in almost every aspect of life will become as natural as turning on the radio or TV or picking up the phone. You will require 'super-Google' search and management engines to find your way around it, and a very smart 'forgettery' to prune and discard material continually from your memory space if complete information overload is to be avoided. It will become increasingly difficult and unthinkable for people to function without continuous access to their personal information spaces. Together with new forms of human capital assessment and accreditation, these might even make old style exams obsolete – providing a perfect record of your lifelong learning and performance, which could be audited by an authorised certification agent, in place of today's examinations and paper qualifications.

Goods and services

This year, eBay will help 30 million people buy $20 billion worth of goods and services. As e-retail services develop further we will be able routinely to send one of our personal agents to get the best deal for us on almost anything we want to procure, from babyfood and clothes to cars, training courses or holidays. When we choose to shop in person – perhaps as an enjoyable leisure activity – the smart devices on our bodies will be able to talk to the screens and displays around the store, and directly to the 'smarts' on every single item in the store.

Disappointingly, nothing like the same attention has been paid to the opportunities for improved delivery of public services, even though productivity here lags far behind the private sector and there is potentially huge value to be added. Current attempts, from online income tax returns to hospital scheduling and combating benefits fraud, however, do not augur well for genuinely ambitious networking approaches to public sector modernisation – or indeed 'e-democracy'. Instant phone referenda may work for *Pop Idol* and *Fame Academy* but serious public issues would not be well served by the same treatment.

Regulating the utility

The information utility will also bring inevitable opportunities for malicious exploitation, and serious vulnerabilities and pathologies, which need to be anticipated and managed. For example, security, privacy and integrity are going to be crucial in this new era. In a world where our interaction with the infrastructure (and with other people and organisations through the infrastructure) is increasingly mediated by trusted agents, brands, identity and authentication will be of great importance. Identity theft and impersonation will have bigger consequences. Conversely, retaining anonymity will become increasingly hard, especially as anonymous cash transactions are replaced by e-transactions, which inevitably leave a trace. If every banknote has its own RFID tag, even cash will lose its anonymity.

This creates unique challenges for regulation. For example, how can you regulate and police a bank that exists only in a computer in a satellite, and delivers its services to you via a wireless link from the infrastructure wherever you are on the planet? Who actually owns it? And when things go wrong, to whom do you complain? Related to this is the question of data accuracy and integrity. One of the few certainties in this future environment is that some of the data held in the world wide utility will be inaccurate, out of date, or just plain wrong, and some will get lost or destroyed. In particular, some of the personal information held about you will be wrong, and we will need quite radical innovations to enable individuals to find out and check, and then get it put it right.

Sometimes this will be due just to malfunctions and accidents. But in other cases there will be deliberate and continuous attempts to subvert and attack the infrastructure for all sorts of criminal, terrorist and other malicious purposes. As a result, we will have to develop processes for continually cross-checking, purging, repairing and restoring data. Like immune systems in living organisms, we will need to counter both ageing from accumulated defects and deliberate infections (such as viruses), as well as the damage to particular components of the system caused by external traumas.

In our contact with the e-world we will rely on trusted third parties with trusted brands to validate the infrastructure for us, and to validate us to it. These will play a key role as the 'super agents' we trust to look after our data and our identity in the face of whatever threats confront the infrastructure. In a world where services can be delivered by anyone from anywhere, trusted brands will be vital. Everything else behind the wall – all the companies, organisations and public institutions – will be virtual, fast changing, elusive and evanescent.

Living in the goldfish bowl

The promise of this new era is immense. The intelligent infrastructure will enable us to manage everything from our personal time to the resources of the whole planet more optimally and effectively. But the threats are also great, not least the risk of complete dependency on the information utility in our personal lives, at work, and when we travel, or attempt to access education, healthcare and other public services. The price of this dependency is that, as individuals, we will have to come to terms with a major surrender of personal privacy. As employees and managers in companies, public institutions and organisations of all kinds, we will face the same issue. Our most confidential emails will be undeletable and the global activities of the organisations we work for will be instantly visible to almost anyone who wants to know. As things become more densely interconnected, time constants and constraints will shrink and we will have less and less chance to think, reflect and make balanced decisions. In short, *we are entering the era of transparency*. This raises important questions concerning how we will cope with living and working in the global goldfish bowl. Will we welcome it and embrace it, or just tolerate it most of the time? Will it be possible to opt out – will we see the emergence of a disaffected 'out-class' on an unprecedented scale?

We will have to use the information infrastructure itself to help us discover, debate and resolve our responses to these challenges. As it grows rapidly larger and more complex than human brains and bodies, that infrastructure will require all of the defence mechanisms evolved by living organisms in order to adapt to and protect themselves from their environments.

One thing is clear: a long wave of disruptive technological innovation is coming. The question is what will it look like and when will it emerge? This cannot be predicted in detail; there is always the possibility of unexpected and even more powerful technologies emerging. But that does not mean that they cannot be shaped by the wider political, economic and social environment. How we incentivise investment in building the infrastructure; how we influence public attitudes to the utility and its impacts; how we manage its legal, ethical and social implications; how we craft the appropriate regulatory framework; all are crucial questions facing developed and developing countries in years to come. Policy-makers and business leaders in the UK must begin to grasp the reality of the era of the information utility if its opportunities, and its threats, are to be appreciated and engaged.

Professor Sir John Taylor completed his five-year term as Director General of Research Councils and Chairman of Research Councils UK in December 2003. He is currently Chairman of Roke Manor Research.

Smart mobs aren't a 'thing' that you can point to with one finger or describe with two words, any more than you could 'the Internet' ...

Smart mobs

Howard Rheingold

DEM☺S

15. Smart mobs

the power of the mobile many

Howard Rheingold

Smart mobs consist of people who are able to act in concert even if they don't know each other. The people who make up smart mobs cooperate in ways never before possible because they carry devices that possess both communication and computing capabilities.

An unanticipated convergence of technologies is suggesting new responses to civilisation's founding question, How can competing individuals learn to work cooperatively? Location-sensing wireless organisers, wireless networks and community supercomputing collectives all have one thing in common: *they enable people to act together in new ways and in situations where collective action was not possible before.*

The 'killer apps' of tomorrow's mobile infocom industry won't be hardware devices or software programmes but social practices. The most far-reaching changes will come, as they often do, from the kinds of relationships, enterprises, communities and markets that the infrastructure makes possible.

Netwar – Dark and Light

On 20 January 2001, President Joseph Estrada of the Philippines became the first head of state in history to lose power to a smart mob. Following the abrupt ending of his impeachment trial by sympathetic senators, Manila residents began to assemble in their thousands on Epifanio de los Santas Avenue (known as 'Edsa'), the site of the 1986

'People Power' peaceful demonstrations that had toppled the Marcos regime. Within 75 minutes, 20,000 people had converged on Edsa, mobilised and coordinated by waves of text messages initiated by opposition leaders: 'Go 2EDSA, Wear blck'. Over four days, more than a million people showed up, mostly dressed in black. The military withdrew support from the regime; the Estrada government fell, as the Marcos regime had fallen a decade previously, largely as a result of massive non-violent demonstrations. The rapid assembly of the anti-Estrada crowd was a hallmark of early smart mob technology, and the millions of text messages exchanged by the demonstrators in 2001 were, by all accounts, a key to the crowd's esprit de corps. The legend of 'Generation Txt' was born.

Bringing down a government without firing a shot was a momentous early eruption of smart mob behaviour. It wasn't, however, the only one.

O On 30 November 1999, autonomous but internet-worked squads of demonstrators protesting at the meeting of the World Trade Organisation (WTO) used 'swarming' tactics, mobile phones, websites, laptops and PDAs to win 'The Battle of Seattle'.

O In September 2000, thousands of citizens in Britain, outraged by a sudden rise in gasoline prices, used mobile phones, SMS, email from laptop PCs and CB radios in taxicabs to coordinate dispersed groups that blocked fuel delivery at selected service stations in a wildcat political protest.

O A violent political demonstration in Toronto in the spring of 2000 was chronicled by a group of roving journalist–researchers who webcast digital video of everything they saw.

O Since 1992, thousands of bicycle activists have assembled monthly for 'Critical Mass' moving demonstrations, weaving through San Francisco streets en masse. Critical Mass operates through loosely linked networks, alerted by mobile phone and email trees, and breaks up into smaller, tele-coordinated groups when appropriate.

The Battle of Seattle saw a more deliberate and tactically focused use of wireless communications and mobile social networks in urban political conflict, more than a year before texting mobs assembled in Manila. A broad coalition of demonstrators who represented different interests but were united in opposition to the views of the World Trade Organisation planned to disrupt the WTO's 1999 meeting in Seattle. The demonstrators included a wide range of different 'affinity groups' who loosely coordinated their actions around their shared objective. The Direct Action Network enabled autonomous groups to choose which levels of action to participate in, from non-violent support to civil disobedience to joining mass arrests – a kind of dynamic ad hoc alliance that wouldn't have been possible without a mobile, many-to-many, real-time communication network. According to a report dramatically titled 'Black flag over Seattle' by Paul de Armond:

> The cohesion of the Direct Action Network was partly due to their improvised communications network assembled out of cell phones, radios, police scanners and portable computers. Protesters in the street with wireless Palm Pilots were able to link into continuously updated web pages giving reports from the streets. Police scanners monitored transmissions and provided some warning of changing police tactics. Cell phones were widely used.[3]

From Seattle to Manila, the first 'netwars' have already broken out. The term 'netwar' was coined by John Arquilla and David Ronfeldt, two analysts for the RAND corporation, who noticed that the same combination of social networks, sophisticated communication technologies, and decentralised organisational structure was surfacing as an effective force in very different kinds of political conflict:

> *Netwar is an emerging mode of conflict in which the protagonists – ranging from terrorist and criminal organisations on the dark side, to militant social activists on the bright side – use network forms of organisation, doctrine, strategy, and technology attuned to the information age…These networks are proving very hard to deal with; some are winning. What all have in common is that they operate in small, dispersed units that can deploy nimbly – anywhere, anytime.[4]*

The 'swarming' strategies noted by Arquilla and Ronfeldt rely on many small units like the affinity groups in the Battle of Seattle. Individual members of each group remained dispersed until mobile communications drew them to converge on a specific location from all directions simultaneously, in coordination with other groups. Manila, Seattle, San Francisco, Senegal and Britain were sites of non-violent political swarming. Arquilla and Ronfeldt cited the non-governmental organisations associated with the Zapatistas movement in Mexico, which mobilised world opinion in support of Indian peasants, and the Nobel Prize-winning effort to enact an anti-landmine treaty as examples of non-violent netwar actions. Armed and violent swarms are another matter. The Chechen rebels in Russia, soccer hooligans in Britain and the FARC guerrillas in Colombia also have used netwar strategy and swarming tactics.[5] The US military is in the forefront of smart mob technology development.

Smart mobs engaging in either violent or non-violent netwar represent only a few of the many possible varieties of smart mob. Netwars do share a similar technical infrastructure with other smart mobs. More importantly, however, they are both animated by a new form of social organisation, the network. Networks include nodes and links, use many possible paths to distribute information from any link to any other, and are self-regulated through flat governance hierarchies and distributed power. Arquilla and Ronfeldt are among many who believe networks constitute the newest major social organisational form, after tribes, hierarchies and markets. Although network-structured communications hold real potential for enabling democratic forms of decision-making and beneficial instances of collective action, that doesn't mean that the transition to networked forms of social organisation will be a pleasant one with uniformly benevolent outcomes. Arquilla and Ronfeldt note the potential for cooperation in examples like the non-governmental organisations that use netwar tactics for public benefit, but they also articulated a strong caution, worth keeping in mind when contemplating the future of smart mobs:

> *Most people might hope for the emergence of a new form of organisation to be led by 'good guys' who do 'the right thing' and grow stronger because of it. But history does not support this contention. The cutting edge in the early rise of a new form may be found equally among malcontents, ne'er-do-wells, and clever opportunists eager to take advantage of new ways to manoeuvre, exploit, and dominate.[6]*

Lovegety and peer-to-peer journalism

In light of the military and terrorist potential of netwar tactics it would be foolish to presume that only benign outcomes should be expected from smart mobs. But any observer who focuses exclusively on the potential for violence would miss evidence of perhaps even more profoundly disruptive potential – for beneficial as well as malign purposes – of smart mob technologies and techniques. Could cooperation epidemics break out if smart mob media spread beyond warriors – to citizens, journalists, scientists, people looking for fun, friends, mates, customers or trading partners?

Consider a few experiments on the fringes of mobile communications that might point towards a wide variety of non-violent smart-mobbing in the future:

O 'Interpersonal awareness devices' have been evolving for several years. Since 1998 hundreds of thousands Japanese have used Lovegety keychain devices that signal when

another Lovegety owner of the opposite sex and
compatible profile is within 15 feet.

o   ImaHima ('are you free now?') enables hundreds of
thousands of Tokyo i-mode users to alert buddies who are
in their vicinity at the moment.

o   Upoc ('universal point of contact') in Manhattan
sponsors mobile communities of interest: any member of
'Manhattan celebrity watch', 'nyc terrorism alert', 'prayer of
the day' or 'The Resistance', for example, can broadcast
text messages to and receive messages from all the other
members.

o   Phones that make it easy to send digital video directly to
the web make it possible for 'peer-to-peer journalism'
networks to emerge; Steve Mann's students in Toronto
have chronicled newsworthy events by webcasting
everything their wearable cameras and microphones
capture.

o   Researchers in Oregon have constructed 'social
middleware' that enables wearable computer users to
form ad hoc communities, using distributed reputation
systems, privacy and knowledge-sharing agents, and
wireless networks.

In 2000 WearComp researcher, innovator and evangelist Steve Mann
launched 'ENGwear, an experiment in wearable news-gathering
systems conducted by students and researchers at the Humanistic
Intelligence Lab at the University of Toronto'.[7] In the spring of 2000
Mann and a group of his students, all wearing computers equipped
with 'EyeTaps', which broadcast everything they saw and heard to the
Web, showed up at a demonstration in Toronto called by the Ontario
Coalition Against Poverty (OCAP). Violence broke out. Mann
reported:

*We, along with the journalists and various television crews, ran
for cover. However, unlike the reporters, my students and I were*

still broadcasting, capturing almost by accident the entire event. Whatever we saw before us was captured and sent instantly in real time to the World Wide Web, without our conscious thought or effort.[8]

Swarm intelligence and the social mind

Massive outbreaks of cooperation precipitated the collapse of communism. In city after city, huge crowds assembled in non-violent street demonstrations, despite decades of well-founded fear of political assembly. Although common sense leads to the conclusion that unanimity of opinion among the demonstrators explained the change of opinion, Natalie Glance and Bernardo Huberman, Xerox PARC researchers who have studied the dynamics of social systems, noted that a diversity of cooperation thresholds among the individuals can tip a crowd into a sudden epidemic of cooperation. Glance and Huberman pointed out that a minority of extremists can choose to act first and, if the conditions are right, their actions can trigger actions by others who needed to see somebody making the first move before acting themselves – at which point the bandwagon-jumpers follow the early adopters who followed the first actors.[9]

Sudden epidemics of cooperation aren't necessarily pleasant experiences. Lynch mobs and entire nations cooperate to perpetrate atrocities. Decades before the fall of communism, sociologist Mark Granovetter examined radical collective behaviour of both positive and negative kinds and proposed a 'threshold model of collective behaviour'. I recognised Granovetter's model as a crucial conceptual bridge that connects intelligent (smart mob) cooperation with 'emergent' behaviours of unintelligent actors, such as hives, flocks and swarms.

Granovetter studied situations in which individuals were faced with either–or decisions regarding their relationship to a group – whether or not to join a riot or strike, adopt an innovation, spread a rumour, sell a stock, leave a social gathering, migrate to a different country. He identified *the pivotal statistic as the proportion of other people who would have to act before an individual decides to join them.*

One of Granovetter's statements yielded a clue to smart mob dynamics: 'By explaining paradoxical outcomes as the result of aggregation processes, threshold models take the "strangeness" often associated with collective behaviour out of the heads of actors and put it into the dynamics of situations.'[10]

Threshold models of collective action are about media for exchange of coordinating knowledge. Understanding this made it possible to see something I had not noticed clearly enough before – a possible connection between computer-wearing social networks of thinking, communicating humans and the swarm intelligence of unthinking (but also communicating) ants, bees, fish, and birds. Individual fish and birds (and tight-formation fighter pilots) school and flock simply by paying attention to what their nearest neighbours do. The coordinated movement of schools and flocks is a dynamically shifting aggregation of individual decisions. Even if there were a central tuna or pigeon who could issue orders, no system of propagating orders from a central source can operate swiftly enough to avoid being eaten by sharks or slamming into trees. When it comes to hives and swarms, the emergent capabilities of decentralised self-organisation can be surprisingly intelligent.

What happens when the individuals in a tightly coordinated group are more highly intelligent creatures rather than simpler organisms like insects or birds? How do humans exhibit emergent behaviour?

Kevin Kelly traced back the new theories regarding emergent properties to William Morton Wheeler, an expert in the behaviour of ants.[11] Wheeler called insect colonies 'superorganisms' and defined the ability of the hive to accomplish tasks that no individual ant or bee is intelligent enough to do on its own as 'emergent properties' of the superorganism. Kelly drew parallels between the ways both biological and artificial 'vivisystems' exhibit the same four characteristics of what he called 'swarm systems':

○   the absence of imposed centralised control
○   the autonomous nature of sub-units
○   the high connectivity between the sub-units

   O   the webby non-linear causality of peers influencing
        peers.[12]

Steven Johnson's 2001 book *Emergence* shows how the principles that
Kelly extrapolated from biological to technological networks also
apply to cities and Amazon.com's recommendation system: 'In these
systems, agents residing on one scale start producing behaviour that
lies on one scale above them: ants create colonies; urbanites create
neighbourhoods; simple pattern-recognition software learns how to
recommend new books. The movement from low-level rules to
higher level sophistication is what we call emergence.'[13] In the case of
cities, although the emergent intelligence resembles the ant mind, the
individual units, humans, possess extraordinary onboard intelligence
– or at least the capacity for it.

At this point, connections between the behaviour of smart mobs
and the behaviour of swarm systems must be tentative, yet several of
the earliest investigations have shown that the right kinds of online
social networks know more than the sum of their parts: connected
and communicating in the right ways, populations of humans can
exhibit a kind of 'collective intelligence'.

There have been various theories about the internet as the nervous
system of a global brain, but Bernardo Huberman and his colleagues
at Hewlett-Packard's Information Dynamics research laboratory have
made clever use of markets and game simulations as computational
test beds for experiments with emergent group intelligence.
Huberman and his colleagues have used 'information markets' to
perform experiments in emergent social intelligence. The Hollywood
Stock Exchange, for example, uses the market created from the
trading of symbolic shares to predict box office revenues and Oscar
winners. They have found that group forecasts were more accurate
than those of any of the individual participants' forecasts.[14] The HP
research team makes the extraordinary claim that they have created a
mathematically verifiable methodology for extracting emergent
intelligence from a group and using the group's knowledge to predict
the future in a limited but useful realm: 'One can take past predictive

performance of participants in information markets and create weighting schemes that will predict future events, even if they are not the same event on which the performance was measured.'[15]

Decades ago, computer scientists thought that some day there would be forms of 'artificial intelligence' but, with the exception of a few visionaries, they never thought in terms of computer-equipped humans as a kind of social intelligence. Although everyone who understands the use of statistical techniques to make predictions hastens to add a disclaimer that surprises are inevitable, and one of the fundamental characteristics of complex adaptive systems is their unpredictability, the initial findings that internet-worked groups of human beings can exhibit emergent prediction capabilities are potentially profound.

Another research group that takes emergent group intelligence seriously is the laboratory at Los Alamos, where a group of 'artificial life' researchers issued a report in 1998, 'Symbiotic intelligence: self-organising knowledge on distributed networks, driven by human interaction'.[16] The premise of this interdisciplinary team is based on the view proposed by some in recent years that human society is an adaptive collective organism and that social evolution parallels and unfolds according to the same dynamics as biological evolution.[17] According to this theory, new knowledge and new technologies have made possible the evolution of the maximum size of the functioning social group from tribes to nations to global coalitions. The knowledge and technology that triggered the jump from clan to tribe to nation to market to network all shared one characteristic: they each amplified the way individual humans think and communicate, and magnified their ability to share what they know.

The research conducted directly by the Los Alamos researchers reinforced Huberman et al's claims that groups of humans, linked through online networks, can make collective decisions that prove more accurate than the performance of the best individual predictors in the group. If it isn't a dead end, the lines of research opened by Huberman's team, the Los Alamos researchers and others could amplify the powers of smart mobs into entirely new dimensions of possibility, the way Moore's Law amplified the powers of computer users.

Conclusion

Will self-organised, ad hoc networks of computer wearers, mediated by privacy-protecting agents, blossom into a renaissance of new wealth, knowledge and revitalised civil society, or will the same technological–social regime provide nothing more than yet another revenue stream for Disinfotainment, Inc.?

Or is that the wrong question? Given the direction of the technological, economic and political changes I have touched on, I propose the following questions:

○ What do we know now about the emergent properties of ad hoc mobile computing networks, and what do we need to know in the future?

○ What are the central issues for individuals in a world pervaded by surveillance devices – in terms of what we can do about it?

○ What are the long-term consequences of near-term political decisions on the way we'll use and be affected by mobile, pervasive, always-on media?

Smart mobs aren't a 'thing' that you can point to with one finger or describe with two words, any more than 'the internet' was a 'thing' you could point to. The internet is what happened when a lot of computers started communicating. The computer and the internet were designed, but the ways people used them were not designed into either technology, nor were the most world-shifting uses of these tools anticipated by their designers or vendors. Word processing and virtual communities, eBay and e-commerce, Google and weblogs and reputation systems *emerged*. Smart mobs are an unpredictable but at least partially describable emergent property that I see surfacing as more people use mobile telephones, more chips communicate with each other, more computers know where they are located, more technology becomes wearable, and more people start using these new media to invent new forms of sex, commerce, entertainment, communion and, as always, conflict.

Howard Rheingold is the author of Smart Mobs: the next social revolution, *from which this essay is extracted.*

Notes

1   V Rafael, 'The cell phone and the crowd: messianic politics in recent Philippine history,' 13 June 2001, available at
    http://communication.ucsd.edu/people/f_rafael.cellphone.html.

2   R Lloyd Parry, 'The TXT MSG revolution', *Independent,* 23 Jan 2001, available at www.independent.co.uk/story.jsp?story=51748 (accessed 1 Mar 2002).

3   P de Armond, 'Black flag over Seattle,' *Albion Monitor* 72, Mar 2000, available at www.monitor.net/monitor/seattlewto/index.html (accessed 1 Mar 2002).

4   D Ronfeldt and J Arquilla, 'Networks, netwars, and the fight for the future,' *First Monday* 6, 10 October (2001),
    http://firstmonday.org/issues/issue6_10/ronfeldt/index.html (accessed 1 Mar 2002).

5   Ibid.

6   J Arquilla and D Ronfeldt (eds) *Networks and Netwars: the future of terror, crime, and militancy* (Santa Monica, Ca: RAND, 2001).

7   'ENGwear: wearable wireless systems for electronic news gathering', available at www.eyetap.org/hi/ENGwear (accessed 1 Mar 2002).

8   S Mann and H Niedzviecki, *Cyborg: digital destiny and human possibility in the age of the wearable computer* (Mississauga: Doubleday Canada, 2001).

9   N Glance and B Huberman, The dynamics of social dilemmas', *Scientific American*, March 1994.

10 M Granovetter, 'Threshold models of collective behaviour', *American Journal of Sociology* 83, no 6 (1978).

11 WM Wheeler, *Emergent Evolution and the Development of Societies* (New York: WW Norton, 1928).

12 Ibid.

13 S Johnson, *Emergence: the connected lives of ants, brains, cities and software* (New York: Scribner, 2001).

14 K Chen, L Fine and B Huberman, 'Forecasting uncertain events with small groups,' HP Laboratories, Palo Alto, California, 3 Aug 2001, http://papers.ssrn.com/sol3/papers.cfm?abstract_id=278601 (accessed 6 March 2002)

15 Ibid.

16 N Johnson et al, 'Symbiotic intelligence: self-organising knowledge on distributed networks, driven by human interaction,' in C Adami et al (eds) *Artificial Life VI: proceedings of the Sixth International Conference on Artificial*

Life (Complex Adaptive Systems, No 6) (Cambridge: Bradford Books/MIT Press, 1998).

17 G Dyson, *Darwin Among the Machines: the evolution of global intelligence* (Reading, MA: Addison-Wesley, 1997).

Social movements have always had an impact on politics. In an increasingly connected society, a new breed – the network campaign – has emerged . . .

The rise of network campaigning

Paul Miller

DEM☉S

16. The rise of network campaigning

Paul Miller

16 May 1998 was the day the network came alive. By coach, car, train, boat, bike and foot, 70,000 people converged on Birmingham where the G8 leaders, the most powerful men on the planet, were meeting in a steel, glass and concrete building especially fortified for the occasion by hundreds of CIA officers. At 3pm, the campaigners formed a human chain some 10km long, encircling the security-cordoned conference centre. But the men and women who had criss-crossed the UK to join hands weren't there to protest about a high-profile issue, decision or event in the news. Instead they wanted to make their feelings known about a complicated and, at the time, obscure matter of economic policy. They were supporters of the Jubilee 2000 campaign to cancel the unpayable debts of the world's poorest nations.

Social movements have always had an important effect on our political systems but in an increasingly connected society a new breed – the network campaign – has emerged. On issues from the environment and human rights to poverty eradication and debt reduction, network campaigns have taken on some of the biggest and most powerful institutions on the planet: from governments and multinational companies to the World Trade Organisation and the World Bank. Connecting non-governmental organisations, faith groups and trade unions as well as individual campaigners, networks have emerged that combine the resources, powers, skills and experience of diverse institutions in new and potent combinations. While there has been no network theorist behind their strategies, campaigners have learned that networks offer a number of advantages over other institutional models. Over time, they have become their weapon of choice.

This essay argues that politics has much to understand and learn about network campaigning. It begins by examining the structure of the network campaigns, then goes on to look at the reasons for the use of networks by campaigners over other organisational forms before looking at some of the downsides network campaigning presents. It draws on examples from the Jubilee 2000 campaign, perhaps the first fully fledged network campaign to reach public consciousness.[1]

The characteristics of network campaigns

First we need to consider what makes a campaign a 'network campaign'. Simple definitions are difficult since it is partly the looseness of institutional structure and the diversity of tactics that make network campaigns different to traditional approaches. In essence, network campaigning allows a diverse grouping of organisations and individuals to participate through commitment to a shared purpose, while remaining autonomous individual agents. In this way it is possible to gain additional leverage over decision-making bodies through the 'multiplier effect' of a coherent message and more efficient deployment of resources and effort, while maintaining the flexibility and energy that more bureaucratic forms of coordination tend to squander. The characteristics and common features of network campaigns include the following features.

Having a shared goal

The main characteristic of campaigning networks is that they have a goal shared by those who are part of the network. As David Ronfeldt says, 'The network form offers its best advantages where the members, as often occurs in civil society, aim to preserve their autonomy and to avoid hierarchical controls, yet have agendas that are interdependent and benefit from consultation and coordination.'[2] The meaning and goal of network campaigns is usually so simple to express and communicate that they are often seen as 'single issue' campaigns. For Jubilee 2000, the shared goal was 'a debt-free start for a billion people'.

Being structure light

Network campaigns tend to be very light on traditional structure with only a small secretariat or coordinating body compared to the size of the network or the resources that it is able to mobilise. The role of the secretariat becomes that of network nurturer. Secretariats must spend their time creating connections between other people, and channelling the energy and enthusiasm that is created in the network towards increasing the cumulative impact on decision-makers. The central secretariat can also help the network to interpret the overall environment for the campaign by providing research and communicating feedback from political targets. Often networks have some form of democratic involvement from members, again coordinated by the secretariat. This can take the form of a management board, with some positions elected by network members and others filled by the founders of the campaign.

Mobilising a coalition of skills and resources

Each of the most prominent examples of networked campaigning over the last decade has drawn on established organisations and linked them together in a coalition of the wilful. Coalition members provide resources to fund the secretariat and access to their memberships and communication channels. However, individuals don't have to be part of one of the coalition organisations to be part of the campaign. There are always easy ways to get involved, from simply signing a petition to show your support, through attending demonstrations, to letting it take over your life as a full-time member of staff or volunteer. The network will also include people with a variety of different skills that can be drawn upon at short notice.

Use of network technology

The internet has been vital to network campaigners and novel uses of the web, email or newsgroups are a common thread through several of the network campaigns of the late 1990s. Technology also plays a key role in recording events and important moments for the campaign. Since it is likely that the central secretariat won't be well enough resourced to be at every local demonstration or meeting, small groups of activists can use technology to swap pictures, video or recordings of events to give a rich picture of the level of activity within the network. The Jubilee 2000 website provided between 8,000 and 12,000 people with up-to-date information about the campaign every week. A webchat with Bono run by Jubilee 2000 in conjunction with MSN received hundreds of thousands of hits.

Embracing diversity and openness

An approach used by network campaigners is to communicate using a variety of different media, each allowing them to connect to new constituencies. So network campaigns don't just rely on, say, producing a magazine or holding a public meeting: they have a variety of ways of communicating to match the variety of potential participants. While it would be very unusual for organisations with completely opposite goals to the rest of the network to be allowed to join, it is not necessary for network members to agree on everything. Network members need to be compatible in their views, not identical. Jubilee 2000 brought together organisations as diverse as Friends of the Earth and the Mother's Union.

Use of celebrity

The power of TV can reach the parts that social networks cannot. In an era of broadcast media concentration and satellite news channels that reach across the world, campaigners have needed a way of accessing and harnessing these networks. The solution they have identified has been to use something that is common currency in these networks – a bit of stardust. When the organisers of the Brit awards decided to promote the Jubilee 2000 campaign after both

Muhammad Ali and Bono said they would attend, their message promoting the campaign reached a global TV audience of over 100 million people as well as widespread coverage in the press.

Use of physical space

The tactic of network campaigners has often been to foster a large and diverse network and then bring as many members of the networks as possible together in one place. The vibrant atmosphere on these occasions does not just look impressive for the TV cameras; it has also given campaigns an additional injection of energy. It has given people the motivation to go away and create new network connections. Jubilee 2000 took the human chain as its symbol of choice when bringing people together.

Personalisation of targets

While campaigners might want to include as many people as possible in their network, they see the value of focusing their efforts on one or two individuals who will feel the full weight of the network's efforts. In the UK, it was Tony Blair and Gordon Brown who took the flak from the Jubilee 2000 campaign. The mail rooms at Number 10 Downing Street and the Treasury discovered first-hand how large the Jubilee 2000 network had become when postcards from the network began to arrive in their tens of thousands.

Being time limited

A sense of urgency is the network campaigners' best friend. Jubilee 2000 took the end of the millennium as a deadline for world leaders to make a decision, taking their inspiration from the biblical idea of jubilee, the time when debts would be forgiven and slaves freed every 50 years. While social links created through one particular network campaign might live on to be used another day, individual network campaigns disappear as quickly as they are created.

Network campaigning 'attractors'

Why has the network become the organisational form of choice for campaigners? One way of understanding this is to look at the advantages that this mode of organisation offers.

It's cheaper

Setting up new institutions is expensive. If you have a cause to fight, the requirements to build an organisational infrastructure able to communicate with millions of people are huge. Network campaigns make up for their shortfall in terms of financial muscle by tapping into the existing infrastructure that large NGOs or civil society organisations already possess. Using these latent networks and institutional resources as much as possible helps to keep costs to a minimum. If they do have a central secretariat at all, network campaigns do not have a large number of paid staff (Jubilee 2000 had at most 25 paid staff and for much of its lifetime even fewer).

It's quicker

A campaign can be built up very quickly through a network when it could have taken decades by other means. This is partly because campaigners don't need to raise as much money, but also because the agreement of a large number of people is not required before doing anything – decision-making structures are usually very light. And once a network has reached a critical mass, the campaign can move very quickly indeed. Like an epidemic, the message spreads (sometimes uncontrollably) through social networks, new connections reinforcing old connections. It took just four years for Jubilee 2000 to grow from being a UK-based organisation with a single employee working out of a shed on London's South Bank to an international force to be reckoned with, with 69 national campaigns and 24 million signatures on its petition.

It provides eyes everywhere

Network campaigns provide an army of researchers sending each other bits of information all the time. In particular, the internet has revolutionised links between campaigners across the globe. On 13 April 2000, 63 campaigners were arrested in Kenya during a debt march. News of their arrest was circulated via the internet, prompting letters of protest from around the world. On 22 May of the same year the charges were dropped. Andre Hotchkiss, one of the arrested marchers said: 'Without the avalanche of email, fax, and letters that poured into Kenya, this thing may have pushed on for a longer time.'

It's more fun

Networks mean meeting new people and developing new friendships, often with people who you would never have come into contact with otherwise. Network campaigners make sure that there are plenty of chances to communicate and meet with others who share their goal. Physical gathering points are usually best, be they church meetings, student activist groups or informal groups meeting in people's homes. The traditional image of campaigns – delivering leaflets on a soggy winter's day, or hanging around at aggressive picket lines – has given way to a more colourful, eye-catching carnival atmosphere where a sense of humour is always present.

Ultimately, it's more effective

Described by Anthony Gaeta, a spokesman for the World Bank, as 'one of the most effective global lobbying campaigns I have ever seen', Jubilee 2000 surprised many of the institutions in the firing line with the sheer energy and enthusiasm they were able to generate.[3] The network not only enabled Jubilee 2000 to bring together 70,000 people for one moment in 1998 or to gather 24 million petition signatures but also put the issue of debt high up on the agenda of subsequent international meetings and resulted in over $36 billion of debts being cancelled. The fact that many of the organisations involved in Jubilee 2000 in the UK are now part of the Trade Justice Movement, a network campaign using many of the tactics of Jubilee 2000 to campaign for fairer trade rules between developed and developing nations, perhaps also shows that they themselves see the advantages of network campaigning for getting results.

The challenges of networks

But networks do have downsides. Accountability, for example, is often messy in networks, not easily corresponding to conventional ideas of due process or democracy. The qualification for inclusion in a network is enthusiasm and a willingness to work with others, but this can develop to a point where the people who are the most enthusiastic and most connected – the hubs – can dominate. These are people who move between established groups, passing on information, encouraging collaboration and fixing meetings. They could be housewives or headmasters, accountants or Baptist ministers and they are vital to the success of network campaigns. But since they are often neither employed nor elected by the campaign they can be very difficult to hold to account. While most network campaigns have some democratic functions built into their very light structures, they can be dogged by allegations that particular personalities are allowed to dominate. Within international networks problems of 'strength of voice' can cause tensions, particularly between campaigners in the South and those in the North. In extreme circumstances, this can lead to a second challenge in campaigning networks – forking. This is a problem also seen in 'open source' software programming, where disagreement over the overall goal or aim of the network leads to it splitting into two or more parts.

Another challenge is that once networks have grown they become harder to maintain. Success can be expensive. As networks become more effective and their activity more visible, traditional political actors such as governments, corporate institutions or the media look for a central point to ask questions and, if they are seeking to quash the network, to focus their firepower. This leads to what some campaigners call 'death by consultation', where the secretariat at the centre is distracted from its central goal of nurturing the network by the need to invest more and more time, people and resources in servicing requests from the outside world. Just at the moment that success in terms of profile has been achieved (a prerequisite for large-scale networks) secretariats can grow very rapidly and demands for the secretariat to become run like a 'normal' organisation grow.

Network campaigns can also burn out before their goals are achieved. Members of the network need to have something they can individually achieve in order to see the value in their activity. But if people see change happening quickly, and their cause getting widespread coverage in the media, they think they've done enough. For this reason network campaigns tend to have a high-water mark – a point where they are at the peak of their influence, when they can do most. After that they can find it hard to survive.

Finally and, looking to the future, perhaps most importantly, is the question of whether network campaigns can become a constructive force for change in their own right, or whether they will remain essentially parasitic on existing institutional structures, policy tools and power bases. Can they learn to deliver solutions to problems, rather than just hoping that by shouting loud enough and long enough they will get solved by someone else? Networks seem to be very good at undermining more traditional organisational forms but, so far, surprisingly few have made the transition to constructing new positive institutions. The criticism levelled at campaigners by governments or multilateral institutions is 'could they do any better?' The World Social Forum is an attempt by a huge swathe of civil society groups to do just this. If successful, it could prove to be a massive step forward for network-based civil society solutions.

The future of network campaigning

So what does the future hold for network campaigning? What will be the longer-term effects of repeated use of network campaigning? Will it influence levels of activity in civil society more broadly, for instance, increasing (or decreasing) membership of more traditional, vertically organised civil society institutions like the large NGOs? If people see the network campaigns as more effective than the institutions they are based upon, will they continue to support those institutions? And are network campaigns getting more effective over time as they learn from previous campaigns? These are all questions to be researched and understood.

But the most important area of development will be in the political domain. Increasing use of network campaigning could pose a significant threat to national governments. We have already seen the potential political power of network campaigns in developing countries.[4] In 2003 the UK Stop The War Coalition brought more than a million people on to the streets of London. If network campaigns continue to grow in terms of their numerical power and the sophistication of campaigning techniques, it could only be a matter of time before a major Western government is brought down by a network campaign. Networks have provided civil society organisations with a way of handling organisational and logistical complexity that governments have yet to embrace.

Political parties themselves will need to learn from the network campaigners. As Manuel Castells has written: 'Mass political parties, when and where they still exist, are empty shells, barely activated as electoral machines at regular intervals.'[5] The rapid shrinkage in the membership of political parties in the UK should be cause for concern, and the simultaneous growth in the prominence of network campaigns offers some lessons for their future. Howard Dean's campaign for the Democratic nomination for the US presidency is the most prominent example to date of putting the techniques of network campaigning to effect. Certainly the Dean network showed many of the characteristics outlined above, and its influence both on the tone and the issues that have defined the present contest, and on the evolution of future campaign strategies, should not be underestimated. That Dean's networks were enough to catapult him from obscurity to front-runner but not, ultimately, to deliver the final prize perhaps also points to the next challenge for network politics: navigating the delicate point where the new grassroots networks come face to face with the old hierarchies of power, influence and communication.

So the final question for the future is: what would happen if a network campaign did successfully propel a government into office? And when it got there, what would it mean for current models of governance? For now, these remain 'what if' questions. Yet the need to shift power and decision-making away from the centre, and the broader task of renewing the legitimacy of parties, government and politics itself, are now an established part of the contemporary debate. As UK Cabinet Office Minister, Douglas Alexander MP has argued: 'Our challenge now is to build on the foundations of the distributive democracy we have begun to fashion.'[6] The campaigns, like Jubilee 2000, that have used networks so effectively in recent years might just hold the key.

Paul Miller is a researcher at Demos.

Notes

1   The UK Jubilee 2000 Coalition closed its doors in December 2000. It has been succeeded in the UK by the Jubilee Debt Campaign and Jubilee Research, both of which continue to advocate the cancellation of unpayable debts of poor countries. Examples in this essay are with thanks to Nick Buxton, formerly of the UK Jubilee 2000 Coalition, and Jess Worth of People and Planet.

2   D Ronfeldt, *Tribes, Institutions, Markets, Networks: a framework about societal evolution* (California: Rand Institute, 1996).

3   Quoted in *PR Week*, 16 April 1999.

4   For more information, see H Rheingold, *Smart Mobs: the next social revolution* (Cambridge, MA: Perseus, 2002).

5   M Castells, *The Internet Galaxy: reflections on the internet, business and society* (Oxford: Oxford University Press, 2002).

6   In foreword to D Rushkoff, *Open Source Democracy: how online communication is changing offline politics* (London: Demos, 2003).

Power does not reside in institutions, not even the state or large corporations. It is located in the networks that structure society . . .

Afterword: why networks matter

Manuel Castells

DEM☉S

17. Afterword

why networks matter

Manuel Castells

According to the insightful essays in this volume, networks appear to be the organising form of life, including social life. If this is the case, why is it only in recent years that networks have come to the forefront of social practice? Why the network society *now*?

The answer is in the development of microelectronics and software-based communication technologies. Of course, we know that technology does not determine society. But we also know that without specific technologies some social structures could not develop. For example, the industrial society could not have emerged without electricity and the electrical engine.

Thus only under the conditions of the recent wave of information and communication technologies could networks (an old form of social organisation) address their fundamental shortcoming: their inability to manage coordination functions beyond a certain threshold of size, complexity and velocity. Only under the electronics-based technological paradigm can networks reconfigure themselves in real time, on a global–local scale, and permeate all domains of social life. This is why we live in a network society, not in an information society or a knowledge society.

Indeed, if by information or knowledge society we mean a society in which information is an essential source of wealth and power, I doubt there is any society in history that escapes this characterisation. If by information society we mean a society in which the technological paradigm is the dominant medium for social organisation, this is our society. But to characterise society only by its technological dimension is reductionist and implicitly deterministic. The proper identification of our society is in terms of its specific social structure: networks powered by microelectronics and software-based information and communication technologies. If this is the case, as a growing body of research seems to indicate, a number of consequences follow.

First, the network society expands on a global scale. This is the structural basis for globalisation. Networks know no boundaries. If there is a material communication infrastructure (such as the internet or an air transportation network) societies become interconnected throughout the world on the basis of multidimensional networks. Furthermore, the networking logic explains the features of the process of globalisation. This is because, as Geoff Mulgan explained to us in his pioneering work more than a decade ago, networks communicate and incommunicate at the same time. So while the network society is organised on a global scale, not all territories, or people, are connected in this network society. But all countries are influenced, shaped and ultimately dominated by the logic, interests and conflicts of this network society – the multidimensional network of networks structuring people's life around the planet – while also being shaped and modified by the codes and programmes inscripted by people's action.

Second, networked organisations outcompete all other forms of organisation, particularly the vertical, rigid, command-and-control bureaucracies. This is how networks expand, for instance, in the business world. Companies that do not or cannot follow this logic are outperformed and ultimately phased out by leaner, more flexible competitors. Yes, we live in a world of mergers and conglomerates, but the succesful ones are precisely those based on networks and flexible partnerships. The image of networked firms is too often associated with small and medium-sized businesses. In reality, it is a much more complex world of large firms internally networked, cooperating with networks of small and medium firms, and integrated in broader, strategic alliances in which cooperation and competition alternate, often with the same actors, in different times and spaces.

Third, the networking of political institutions is the de facto response to the management crisis suffered by nation states in a supranational world. The call for global governance has been answered to some extent in the practice of governments and social actors. Not under the utopian form of a world government led by retired statesmen and noble intellectuals, but in the daily practice of joint decision-making in a network state made of nation-states, supranational associations, international institutions, local and regional governments, and quasi-public non-governmental organisations.

Fourth, civil society is reconstructed at the local and global level through networks of activists, often organised and debated over the internet, which form and reconfigure depending on issues, on events, on moods, on cultures. The network society does not cease to be a contradictory structure, and a conflictual practice, as all societies in history have been.

Fifth, sociability is transformed in the new historical context, with networked individualism emerging as the synthesis between the affirmation of an individual-centred culture, and the need and desire for sharing and co-experiencing. Virtual communities and smart mobs, hybrid networks of space and photons (as in the ME++ culture conceptualised by William Mitchell) are redefining space and time not in the terms of the science fiction writers but as the appropriation of technology by people for their own uses and values.

Sixth, the whole range of social practices, both global and local, communicates in the media space. The media, in the broadest sense, are the public space of our time: the space in which, and by which, societies exist as social forms of shared experience. Not just the mainstream media, but all media, the hypertext formed by television, radio, the print press, movies, music, videogames, art – and the internet as the communication medium of all the communication media. The elasticity and interactivity of the media hypertext, its recombinant power, provide the media space with infinite capacity to integrate and to exclude, thus defining the boundaries of society in the material world of our minds and representations.

Finally, in this network society, power continues to be the fundamental structuring force of its shape and direction. But power does not reside in institutions, not even in the state or in large corporations. It is located in the networks that structure society. Or, rather, in what I propose to call the 'switchers'; that is, the mechanisms connecting or disconnecting networks on the basis of certain programmes or strategies. For instance, in the connection between the media and the political system. Or between the financial markets and the regulatory agencies. Or between the criminal economy and the same financial markets. Or between religious apparatuses and government leaders. Or any multi-pronged combination of any of the previous combinations.

Power elite? Precisely not. Elites change with each reconfiguration of networks. Power is exercised by specific configurations of these networks that express dominant interests and values, but whose actors and forms can change. This is why to challenge a certain group in government or in business does not alter the structural logic of domination. This is why to counter networks of power and their connections, alternative networks need to be introduced: networks that disrupt certain connections and establish new ones, such as disconnecting political institutions from the business-dominated media and re-anchoring them in civil society through horizontal communication networks. Networks versus networks. Domination can hardly be exercised against self-configurating networks. And democratic control is lost in a global network of multidimensional domination hidden in the complexity of switches.

Networks matter because they are the underlying structure of our lives. And without understanding their logic we cannot change their programmes to harness their flexibility to our hopes, instead of relentlessly adapting ourselves to the instructions received from their unseen codes. Networks are the Matrix.

Manuel Castells is Wallis Annenberg Chair of Communication Technology and Society, Annenberg School of Communication, University of Southern California, Los Angeles.

DEMOS – Licence to Publish

THE WORK (AS DEFINED BELOW) IS PROVIDED UNDER THE TERMS OF THIS LICENCE ("LICENCE"). THE WORK IS PROTECTED BY COPYRIGHT AND/OR OTHER APPLICABLE LAW. ANY USE OF THE WORK OTHER THAN AS AUTHORIZED UNDER THIS LICENCE IS PROHIBITED. BY EXERCISING ANY RIGHTS TO THE WORK PROVIDED HERE, YOU ACCEPT AND AGREE TO BE BOUND BY THE TERMS OF THIS LICENCE. DEMOS GRANTS YOU THE RIGHTS CONTAINED HERE IN CONSIDERATION OF YOUR ACCEPTANCE OF SUCH TERMS AND CONDITIONS.

1. **Definitions**
   a **"Collective Work"** means a work, such as a periodical issue, anthology or encyclopedia, in which the Work in its entirety in unmodified form, along with a number of other contributions, constituting separate and independent works in themselves, are assembled into a collective whole. A work that constitutes a Collective Work will not be considered a Derivative Work (as defined below) for the purposes of this Licence.
   b **"Derivative Work"** means a work based upon the Work or upon the Work and other pre-existing works, such as a musical arrangement, dramatization, fictionalization, motion picture version, sound recording, art reproduction, abridgment, condensation, or any other form in which the Work may be recast, transformed, or adapted, except that a work that constitutes a Collective Work or a translation from English into another language will not be considered a Derivative Work for the purpose of this Licence.
   c **"Licensor"** means the individual or entity that offers the Work under the terms of this Licence.
   d **"Original Author"** means the individual or entity who created the Work.
   e **"Work"** means the copyrightable work of authorship offered under the terms of this Licence.
   f **"You"** means an individual or entity exercising rights under this Licence who has not previously violated the terms of this Licence with respect to the Work, or who has received express permission from DEMOS to exercise rights under this Licence despite a previous violation.
2. **Fair Use Rights.** Nothing in this licence is intended to reduce, limit, or restrict any rights arising from fair use, first sale or other limitations on the exclusive rights of the copyright owner under copyright law or other applicable laws.
3. **Licence Grant.** Subject to the terms and conditions of this Licence, Licensor hereby grants You a worldwide, royalty-free, non-exclusive, perpetual (for the duration of the applicable copyright) licence to exercise the rights in the Work as stated below:
   a to reproduce the Work, to incorporate the Work into one or more Collective Works, and to reproduce the Work as incorporated in the Collective Works;
   b to distribute copies or phonorecords of, display publicly, perform publicly, and perform publicly by means of a digital audio transmission the Work including as incorporated in Collective Works;
   The above rights may be exercised in all media and formats whether now known or hereafter devised. The above rights include the right to make such modifications as are technically necessary to exercise the rights in other media and formats. All rights not expressly granted by Licensor are hereby reserved.
4. **Restrictions.** The licence granted in Section 3 above is expressly made subject to and limited by the following restrictions:
   a You may distribute, publicly display, publicly perform, or publicly digitally perform the Work only under the terms of this Licence, and You must include a copy of, or the Uniform Resource Identifier for, this Licence with every copy or phonorecord of the Work You distribute, publicly display, publicly perform, or publicly digitally perform. You may not offer or impose any terms on the Work that alter or restrict the terms of this Licence or the recipients' exercise of the rights granted hereunder. You may not sublicence the Work. You must keep intact all notices that refer to this Licence and to the disclaimer of warranties. You may not distribute, publicly display, publicly perform, or publicly digitally perform the Work with any technological measures that control access or use of the Work in a manner inconsistent with the terms of this Licence Agreement. The above applies to the Work as incorporated in a Collective Work, but this does not require the Collective Work apart from the Work itself to be made subject to the terms of this Licence. If You create a Collective Work, upon notice from any Licencor You must, to the extent practicable, remove from the Collective Work any reference to such Licensor or the Original Author, as requested.
   b You may not exercise any of the rights granted to You in Section 3 above in any manner that is primarily intended for or directed toward commercial advantage or private monetary

compensation. The exchange of the Work for other copyrighted works by means of digital file-sharing or otherwise shall not be considered to be intended for or directed toward commercial advantage or private monetary compensation, provided there is no payment of any monetary compensation in connection with the exchange of copyrighted works.

c   If you distribute, publicly display, publicly perform, or publicly digitally perform the Work or any Collective Works, You must keep intact all copyright notices for the Work and give the Original Author credit reasonable to the medium or means You are utilizing by conveying the name (or pseudonym if applicable) of the Original Author if supplied; the title of the Work if supplied. Such credit may be implemented in any reasonable manner; provided, however, that in the case of a Collective Work, at a minimum such credit will appear where any other comparable authorship credit appears and in a manner at least as prominent as such other comparable authorship credit.

5.   Representations, Warranties and Disclaimer

a   By offering the Work for public release under this Licence, Licensor represents and warrants that, to the best of Licensor's knowledge after reasonable inquiry:

   i   Licensor has secured all rights in the Work necessary to grant the licence rights hereunder and to permit the lawful exercise of the rights granted hereunder without You having any obligation to pay any royalties, compulsory licence fees, residuals or any other payments;

   ii   The Work does not infringe the copyright, trademark, publicity rights, common law rights or any other right of any third party or constitute defamation, invasion of privacy or other tortious injury to any third party.

b   EXCEPT AS EXPRESSLY STATED IN THIS LICENCE OR OTHERWISE AGREED IN WRITING OR REQUIRED BY APPLICABLE LAW, THE WORK IS LICENCED ON AN "AS IS" BASIS, WITHOUT WARRANTIES OF ANY KIND, EITHER EXPRESS OR IMPLIED INCLUDING, WITHOUT LIMITATION, ANY WARRANTIES REGARDING THE CONTENTS OR ACCURACY OF THE WORK.

6.   Limitation on Liability. EXCEPT TO THE EXTENT REQUIRED BY APPLICABLE LAW, AND EXCEPT FOR DAMAGES ARISING FROM LIABILITY TO A THIRD PARTY RESULTING FROM BREACH OF THE WARRANTIES IN SECTION 5, IN NO EVENT WILL LICENSOR BE LIABLE TO YOU ON ANY LEGAL THEORY FOR ANY SPECIAL, INCIDENTAL, CONSEQUENTIAL, PUNITIVE OR EXEMPLARY DAMAGES ARISING OUT OF THIS LICENCE OR THE USE OF THE WORK, EVEN IF LICENSOR HAS BEEN ADVISED OF THE POSSIBILITY OF SUCH DAMAGES.

7.   Termination

a   This Licence and the rights granted hereunder will terminate automatically upon any breach by You of the terms of this Licence. Individuals or entities who have received Collective Works from You under this Licence, however, will not have their licences terminated provided such individuals or entities remain in full compliance with those licences. Sections 1, 2, 5, 6, 7, and 8 will survive any termination of this Licence.

b   Subject to the above terms and conditions, the licence granted here is perpetual (for the duration of the applicable copyright in the Work). Notwithstanding the above, Licensor reserves the right to release the Work under different licence terms or to stop distributing the Work at any time; provided, however that any such election will not serve to withdraw this Licence (or any other licence that has been, or is required to be, granted under the terms of this Licence), and this Licence will continue in full force and effect unless terminated as stated above.

8.   Miscellaneous

a   Each time You distribute or publicly digitally perform the Work or a Collective Work, DEMOS offers to the recipient a licence to the Work on the same terms and conditions as the licence granted to You under this Licence.

b   If any provision of this Licence is invalid or unenforceable under applicable law, it shall not affect the validity or enforceability of the remainder of the terms of this Licence, and without further action by the parties to this agreement, such provision shall be reformed to the minimum extent necessary to make such provision valid and enforceable.

c   No term or provision of this Licence shall be deemed waived and no breach consented to unless such waiver or consent shall be in writing and signed by the party to be charged with such waiver or consent.

d   This Licence constitutes the entire agreement between the parties with respect to the Work licensed here. There are no understandings, agreements or representations with respect to the Work not specified here. Licensor shall not be bound by any additional provisions that may appear in any communication from You. This Licence may not be modified without the mutual written agreement of DEMOS and You.